Your

Extraordinary

Life

With excited about
your new life in
Christ Pastors Bill & Joni

Your
Extraordinary
Life

Mark and Patti Virkler

BRIDGE
LOGOS

Newberry, FL 32669

Bridge-Logos

Newberry, FL 32669

Your Extraordinary Life

by Mark and Patty Virkler

Printed in the United States of America.

International Standard Book Number: 978-1-61036-900-8

Library of Congress Catalog Card Number: 2017947786

Unless otherwise noted, scripture quotations are taken from the New American Standard Bible® (NASB), Copyright © 1960, 1962, 1963, 1968, 1971, 1972, 1973, 1975, 1977, 1995 by The Lockman Foundation Used by permission. www.Lockman.org

Cover/Interior designed by Kent Jensen | knail.com

VP 10-15-17

Contents

A Party in Heaven

Did you know that when you decided to follow Jesus, the angels threw a party in Heaven? It's true! They were so excited to know that you had returned to your Father and were going to be spending eternity with them that they just had to have a celebration. (Luke 15:10)

THE LOST ONES

Jesus told three stories about how God feels whenever one of His children finds their way back to Him: the lost sheep, the lost coin and the lost son. The first story talks about a man who has 100 sheep. Every day he takes his sheep out to the hillside where they can graze on plenty of tender sweet grass. Nearby is a quiet little stream where they can drink without danger of being swept away. The shepherd stands guard to be sure that no wild animal attacks them. But one day, one of the sheep wanders too far. He doesn't mean to get into trouble. He isn't trying to run away. He just has his head down, enjoying the meadow and following his nose. "This is really good grass. Ooooh, up ahead there's a nice patch of clover! Yum! Hey, that looks good over there." And before he knows what is happening, he has lost sight of where he started and he doesn't know where he is or how he got there.

Thankfully, the shepherd knows and loves all his sheep individually, so he soon notices that this one is not where he should be. He leaves the 99 other sheep in a safe place and goes out searching. He looks in the thickets, among the rock piles and across the stream. Finally he finds him, far off the path in a waterless, dangerous place. He is so thrilled to find him that picks up that sheep and joyfully carries him on his shoulders all the way back to the rest of the flock. When he gets home that evening, he is still so happy that he calls all his friends and neighbors together to celebrate with him because he found his lost sheep.

Jesus says, "I tell you that in the same way, there will be joy in Heaven over one sinner who repents..." (Luke 15:3-7)!

The next story is about a woman who had ten silver coins. One day while she was looking at them, one fell and rolled away under the furniture and into a dark corner. The coin didn't try to get away from the woman; it was just powerless to resist the circumstances. But the coin was important to the woman so she lit a lamp, got out her broom, and searched carefully through her whole house until she found it. When she did, she called together all her friends and neighbors to celebrate with her because she had found her lost coin.

And Jesus says, "In the same way, I tell you, there is joy in the presence of the angels of God over one sinner who repents" (Luke 15:8-10)!

In the third story, a man had two sons. One day, the younger son decided he was tired of waiting for his father to die before he was able to spend his inheritance having fun and doing the things he wanted to do. So he demanded his share of the estate from his father and took off. He couldn't wait to get far away from the responsibilities and restrictions of his home. When he arrived at a distant country, he really let loose. He threw parties every night for his new "friends," each one wilder than the last. Before long, his money was gone, and so were his friends. A famine hit the land where he was living and he became totally destitute and impoverished. The only job he could find was feeding disgusting, unclean pigs. He was so hungry that even the pods he was feeding to the pigs looked good to him. But no one would give him a thing.

His stomach was growling, his clothes were in rags, he was tired, and he smelled terrible. Finally he came to his senses. "What am I doing here? The servants in my father's house have plenty to eat and here I am dying of hunger! I'm going home. I'd rather be a hired hand in my father's field where at least I will be fed than here among strangers who don't care anything about me." So he headed for home.

But his father had really missed him and was watching the roads, hoping that someday he would see his beloved son returning to him. Finally, there he was! Even though he was still a long way away, his father recognized him and knew that he was on his way home. The father ran out to meet him and hugged him close, kissing him and welcoming him back. He called to the servants to bring him new clothes and to prepare food for a big party so they could celebrate his son that was dead and had come back to life again, who was lost and had been found (Luke 15:11-24).

You may have been like the lost sheep, not deliberately turning your back on God but just wandering away, seeking the things you thought would make you happy, enjoying the pleasures of life, blindly drifting along until you found yourself alone, lost, empty and afraid. Or you might have been like the lost coin, feeling pressured by circumstances you couldn't control and didn't know how to resist, until you were lost in the dark and you felt like no one could see you. Or maybe you were like the lost son, knowing right from wrong, raised in the ways of God, but you wanted to be free from rules and responsibilities and do whatever you wanted, until your life was a mess and nothing seemed worthwhile anymore. It doesn't matter how you became lost; it only matters that now you are found! You are home and all of Heaven is rejoicing!

A CHILD OF GOD

The sinful actions and attitudes that had separated you from God and caused so many problems in your life were washed away by the blood of Jesus. He made you pure and holy and flawless in His sight. On the cross, Jesus took all of your sin and gave you all of His righteousness in exchange. When you received Jesus as your Lord and Savior, He clothed you in a shining robe of righteousness. When God looks at you, He sees perfection! He makes the choice that He will never again remember your sins and lawless actions (Heb. 8:12, Heb. 10:17). In the eyes of God, you have a totally clean slate. You are born again!

"To all who received Him, to those who believed in His name, He gave the right to become children of God"
(JOHN 1:12 BEREAN STUDY BIBLE)

When you received Jesus, when you embraced Him for all that He is, He embraced you as a child of God! The Heavenly Father became your very own loving Father Who cares for you, provides for you and tenderly watches over you. Jesus is your Elder Brother who has promised to never leave you or forsake you. And all other believers in Him became your brothers and sisters.

HIS SPIRIT WITHIN YOU

When you became a child of God, the Holy Spirit came to live inside you, uniting with your spirit so that you became a brand new creation (Acts 2:38, 1 Cor. 6:17). You are a partaker of the divine nature (2 Pet. 1:4). You are not a mere human anymore; you are born again as a child of God!

The Holy Spirit places within you a deep inward conviction that you have been adopted as a child of God - a conviction which prompts you to cry aloud, "Father! Daddy! Papa!" (Rom. 8:15). The Spirit Himself bears witness with your spirit and provides the evidence that you are a child of God (Rom. 8:16). And if you are a child, then you are an heir of God and co-heir with Christ (Rom. 8:17)! His presence in your life is the proof that you have been adopted into God's family (Eph. 1:13, 14, 2 Cor. 1:22). You have been given everything you need to live the life of a child of God (2 Pet. 1:3).

Jesus said the Holy Spirit would be like a river of living water flowing from your innermost being (Jn. 7:37-39). Deep down inside, you sensed a change when the Holy Spirit came to live within you. Righteousness, peace and joy began to bubble up and out, becoming your new way of living (Rom. 14:17). Old things have passed away and fresh new things have come (2 Cor. 5:17).

WELCOME TO THE FAMILY!

We want to help you understand your new family so you feel welcome and comfortable. There are values and behaviors that set us apart and make us different than other people, and there are incredible benefits available to God's children that you have not even imagined (Eph. 3:20). In fact, Jesus came to give you an abundant, uncommon, extraordinary, remarkable life (John 10:10), and we are here to explain some of the things you can do to begin to enjoy that amazing life He promised.

The Bible encourages us to "grow in grace and in the knowledge of our Lord and Savior Jesus Christ" (2 Pet. 3:18). "Grace" is a very important word to Christians and we will be talking about many different ways for you to grow in grace in future chapters. As you walk with the Lord, you will develop a deeper understanding of what "grace" is, but for now, it is enough to know that it refers to God placing within you the desire to please Him and do His will, as well as the strength and ability to do so (Phil. 2:13).

You might have noticed that we keep referring to the Bible (all those references in parentheses). That's because the Bible is the "operations manual" for believers. When we tell you something, we want you to know that it is not just something we have thought up ourselves but it has the authority of God's Word behind it. You can always go to the Bible yourself to confirm that what we have said is true and to find out more.

Personal Application

Write out your answers to these questions so you can share them and return to them to review what the Lord says to you.

1. Ask the Lord to speak to you through His Word, the Bible. Slowly read and think about the following verses. Open the eyes of your heart and ask the Holy Spirit to use your imagination to show you what they are trying to convey to you.

*If we confess our sins, He is faithful and righteous to **forgive** us our sins and to cleanse us from all unrighteousness.*

(1 JOHN 1:9)

*"THEIR SINS AND THEIR LAWLESS DEEDS **I WILL REMEMBER NO MORE.**"* (HEBREWS 10:17)

*As far as the east is from the west, So far has **He removed our transgressions from us**.* (PSALM 103:12)

He will again have compassion on us;
He will tread our iniquities under foot.
*Yes, **You will cast all their sins***
Into the depths of the sea. (MICAH 7:19)

God says that He has forgiven you and cleansed you. He has removed your sins from you "as far as the east is from the west," that He has thrown all your sins "into the depths of the sea," and He "will remember them no more." What does that mean to you, personally? How does that truth change the way you look at yourself and your future?

_____

_____

_____

_____

_____

2. Slowly read through the following verses, really looking at what they say about you. Open the eyes of your heart and ask the Holy Spirit to use your imagination to show you what they are trying to convey to you. Ask the Lord to speak to you through His Word, the Bible.

*He made Him who knew no sin to be sin on our behalf, so that **we might become the righteousness of God in Him**.*

(2 CORINTHIANS 5:21)

*Therefore, **if anyone is in Christ, he is a new creation**. The old has passed away; behold, the new has come.*

(2 CORINTHIANS 5:17 ESV)

*...He has granted to us His precious and magnificent promises, so that by them **you may become partakers of the divine nature**, having escaped the corruption that is in the world by lust.*   (2 PETER 1:4)

*I will rejoice greatly in the LORD, My soul will exult in my God; For He has clothed me with garments of salvation, **He has wrapped me with a robe of righteousness**, As a bridegroom decks himself with a garland, And as a bride adorns herself with her jewels.*   (ISAIAH 61:10)

*For you were formerly darkness, but now **you are Light in the Lord**; walk as children of Light.*   (EPHESIANS 5:8)

Take some time to think about how God sees you right now. Ask Him to open the eyes of your heart to show you yourself as He sees you—pure, holy, flawless, wearing the shining white robe of righteousness. What does that mean to you? How does that change your picture of yourself?

_____

_____

_____

_____

_____

3. Take time to prayerfully read the following verses, asking the Lord to speak to you through them.

> *"To all who received Him, to those who believed in His name, He gave the right to become **children of God**"*
>
> (JOHN 1:12 BEREAN STUDY BIBLE).

> *But when the fullness of the time came, God sent forth His Son, born of a woman, born under the Law, so that He might redeem those who were under the Law, that **we might receive the adoption as sons**. Because you are sons, God has sent forth the Spirit of His Son into our hearts, crying, "Abba! Father!" **Therefore, you are no longer a slave, but a son**; and if a son, then an heir through God.*
>
> (GALATIANS 4:4-7)

> *For you have not received a spirit of slavery leading to fear again, but you have received a spirit of adoption as sons by which we cry out, "Abba! Father!" The Spirit Himself testifies with our spirit that **we are children of God, and if children, heirs also**, heirs of God and fellow heirs with Christ, if indeed we suffer with Him so that we may also be glorified with Him.* (ROMANS 8:15-17)

> *He predestined us to **adoption as sons through Jesus Christ to Himself**, according to the kind intention of His will,*
>
> (EPHESIANS 1:5)

> *For **you are all sons of God through faith in Christ Jesus**.*
>
> (GALATIANS 3:26)

What does it mean to you to be adopted as a child of God? What does it mean to God to have you adopted into His family as His own chosen child? Were you a slave to any habits or sins before you received Christ? What is God's promise to you as His child?

_____

_____

_____

_____

_____

4. King David said, "Your word I have treasured in my heart, that I may not sin against you" (Psalm 119:11). Begin now to treasure God's word in your heart. Choose one of the verses you meditated on in the previous questions, or any verse from Chapter 1 that especially spoke to you. Write it down where you can see it often. Think about it throughout your day. Personalize it. (For example: 2 Corinthians 5:17—I am in Christ, so I am a new creation. The old has passed away; behold, the new has come.) Memorize it so that the truth becomes part of the way you think about yourself.

GROUP ACTIVITIES

1. Share your answers to questions 1–3.

2. The members of the group are now brothers and sisters, part of the family of God. Talk about what that means, practically speaking.

3. Share the verses that you memorized. Talk about why you chose that verse, what it means to you, and any way the Lord has used that verse to help you.

2

Our Lord and Savior

For God so loved the world that He gave His only Son, that whoever believes in Him should not perish but have everlasting life.   (JOHN 3:16)

If you have never heard any other verse in the Bible, you have probably heard John 3:16. Christians like to quote it because it so beautifully sums up the salvation story. It all starts with God's love. The Bible says that "God is love" (1 Jn. 4:8), which means that the essence of Who He is and how He acts is always love. You have become part of a family whose greatest core value is love. Your spirit has personally been united with the Spirit of love. You are loved more than you can even understand—no matter where you live, no matter who you are, no matter what you've done— you are loved beyond measure. You are loved with an everlasting love (Jer. 31:3).

You were created by God to have fellowship with Him. After He created Adam and Eve, God would come and walk with them in the Garden, talking with them about their lives, their work, and their day. He was the Source of life and wisdom within them, teaching and guiding them. His heart was broken when they listened to the Enemy and chose to "be like God" themselves rather than depending on Him and living out of their relationship with Him.

All the good things He had planned for them were forfeited because of their actions. The Garden could no longer be their home. Their labor would no longer be blessed by His hand but would be hard and wearisome. The fruit of their efforts would not joyfully spring forth from the ground but would be resisted and hindered by thorns and thistles. Even the joy of bringing forth children would be shadowed by pain and sorrow. The decisions they made led to sadness, brokenness and death, but most tragically, separation from their God. How different their lives would be from what He created them for—just because they wanted to do it themselves.

And God's heart was broken when you lived apart from Him, too. He saw your attempts to find pleasure and fulfillment apart from Him and He tried to show you how impossible that was. He saw the consequences of your bad decisions and He hurt with your pain. He called to you when you were far from Him to tell you that He had provided a way for you to come home to Him. Because God loved you so much, He gave Jesus, His only Son, to die a horrible death on the cross to take the punishment for your sin. He endured the agony of Hell so that you don't have to. Then God brought Him back to life and many people saw Him alive again—teaching, eating and drinking—until He returned to His throne in Heaven.

WHOEVER BELIEVES IN HIM

All God asks is that we believe in Jesus. It is not enough to believe He was just a great teacher or a good moral example or a holy man. It is not enough to set Him as one among many gods or prophets or sons of God. Jesus is the only First-Born Eternal Son of God. He is fully God and at the same time He is fully man. This is a mystery and a miracle that we cannot understand but it is true nevertheless. He is our Savior, the King and Lord over all (Rev. 19:16, Dan. 4:17, Ps. 103:19).

But it is not enough to simply accept these facts. Even Satan and his demons know those things are true—probably better than we do! So God doesn't say those who believe the truth about Jesus will have eternal life; it is those who believe *in* Jesus. That means that we are willing to commit our lives to Him, trusting Him to be our Savior, our King and our Lord.

We accept that we can do nothing to save ourselves. No matter how many good works we do, we can never earn our way into God's family. No amount of penance or sacrifice on our part can ever satisfy divine justice, because we are merely humans. Nothing we do from the sinful, mortal side can ever bridge the gap to the holy Immortal side. Only God could accomplish our redemption, and He has, in Jesus Christ! We throw ourselves upon Him for salvation, believing and trusting that what He says He has done, He truly *has* done. He has paid for our sins, adopted us into His family, sent the Holy Spirit to live in our hearts, provided all we need to live a holy life, and prepared an eternal home where we will live with Him forever. He is our Savior!

And He continues to be our Savior after we have accepted His forgiveness for our past sins. While God totally cleanses us and makes us new creations when we receive Him, sometimes we give in to the temptations of our old man and sin again. When that happens to you, remember that God loves you and He is your Savior. Don't try to work your way back into His presence by being "extra good." Don't try to hide from Him in shame or embarrassment because you failed to live the way you believe He wants you to. Don't withdraw from Him in guilt over your weakness and failure.

"As a father has compassion on his children, so the Lord has compassion on those who fear Him; for He knows how we are formed, He remembers that we are dust...But from everlasting to everlasting the Lord's love is with those who fear Him..." (Ps. 103:13-17 NIV). "If we confess our sins, he is faithful and righteous to forgive us our sins and cleanse us from all unrighteousness" (1 Jn. 1:8). As soon as you know that you have sinned, run to Him for forgiveness and cleansing. The same faith in the power of Christ's blood that gave you salvation will keep you clean and holy.

our Lord and savior, Jesus Christ

Believing in Jesus is more than receiving Him as our Savior; we must also receive Him as our Lord (2 Pet. 3:18). In our modern culture, we have somewhat lost the meaning of the word "lord," which is "one who has authority, power or control over others, such as a monarch, master or ruler." Especially as Americans, we pride ourselves in our rugged individualism and our independence, arrogantly denying that anyone has control over us and the only authority anyone else has is what we give them. But whether we recognize Him or not, Jesus is the King over all kings and the Lord over all lords (Rev. 19:16). He is the ruler over the realm of mankind and His sovereignty reigns over all (Dan. 4:17, Ps. 103:19).

Believing in Jesus as Lord means that you make Him your Lord, your King, your Master (Matt. 7:21). His will becomes your will. You live only to please and obey Him. You not only give Him the right to direct your life, you actively seek His direction and wisdom. You find out what He wants you to do and you do it. It is your joy to please Him in any way you can. You submit yourself to His authority and choose to no longer insist on doing things your way but rather choose to follow His way.

And really, why wouldn't you want to follow His guidance in every area of your life? This is the all-powerful, all-knowing God we are talking about! He knows the end from the beginning (Is. 46:10). He knows the consequences of every possible decision you could make. He knows where every path you could choose will lead you. And He loves you exceedingly and extravagantly, which means He wants you to have a remarkable, extraordinary life, full of joy, peace and love. If you will listen to Him and obey His leading, He will guide you on a path that leads to a future of hope and abundance, more blessed than you have ever imagined (Jer. 29:11, Jn. 10:10, Eph. 3:20).

In every area you make Him your Lord, He becomes your Savior and you experience heaven on earth in that area of your life. In Scripture, Jesus is always referred to as our "Lord and Savior," never our "Savior and Lord." Lordship comes first. So to the degree that He is Lord of your relationships, He's the Savior of them and they are blessed and peaceful. To the degree He is the Lord of your finances, He is the Savior of your finances and you prosper. To the degree that He is Lord of your body as His temple and you eat and drink to His glory, He saves your body and you experience health and strength—heaven in your body.

THE KINGDOM OF GOD

When you submit to Jesus as your King, you become part of the Kingdom of God, the Kingdom where Love rules. Everything is different here than in the kingdom you used to be part of. Here, the last shall be first and the first last (Matt. 20:16). Here, the meek shall inherit the earth (Matt. 5:5). Here, the greatest among you will be your servant (Matt. 23:11). Here, the foolish things of the world shame the wise and the weak shame the strong (1 Cor. 1:27). And here is peace that transcends all understanding (Phil. 4:7). Here is an inexpressible and glorious joy (1 Pet. 1:8). Here is everlasting love (Jer. 31:3).

So when people ask you why you are so full of joy and peace and hope, and why you don't talk or act the way you used to, you tell them that you are a follower of Jesus because you have discovered that He is the only true Master of the Universe and now He is Master of your life, too (Matt. 10:32, Luke 12:8).

ADDITIONAL RESOURCES

* *The Father Heart of God*—Floyd McClung
* *He Loves Me!*—Wayne Jacobsen
* *Experiencing The Father's Embrace*—Jack Frost
* *From the Father's Heart*—Charles Slagle

PERSONAL APPLICATION

1. *"Not everyone who says to Me, 'Lord, Lord,' will enter the kingdom of heaven, but he who does the will of My Father who is in heaven will enter.*   (MATTHEW 7:21)

    What does it mean to you personally that you have made Jesus your Lord and Savior?

    _____

    _____

    _____

2. Is there any area of your life that you have been struggling to give Jesus full authority over? As you have learned more about His great love for you, are you ready to give it over to Him to control now? If you are, tell Him about it.

    _____

    _____

    _____

    _____

    _____

3. Is there anything in your life that you are not yet willing to give Jesus full authority over? Why are you holding onto it? Are you afraid of what Jesus will tell you to do if you give it to Him? Remember how much He loves you? He only wants what is best for you!

    _____

    _____

    _____

    _____

    Or are you holding onto something that gives you pleasure, even though you know it is wrong? Are you exchanging short-term pleasure for the long-term joy that Jesus promises to those who obey Him? Is that really what you want to do?

    _____

    _____

    _____

    _____

Ask the Lord to show you any areas you are holding onto and why you are so protective of them. Ask Him to make you willing to give them to Him. Remember, He promised that it is His Spirit within you giving you both the desire and the ability to live a godly life. He is there to help you.

4. Choose one of the verses below or any other verse from the chapter to memorize. Filling the "hard drive" of your mind and heart with the Scriptures changes you from the inside out, and that is what Christianity is all about.

"I have loved you with an everlasting love;
Therefore I have drawn you with lovingkindness."

(JEREMIAH 31:3)

The Most High is ruler over the realm of mankind

(DANIEL 4:17)

And on His robe and on His thigh He has a name written,
"KING OF KINGS, AND LORD OF LORDS."

(REVELATION 19:16)

The LORD has established His throne in the heavens, And His sovereignty rules over all. (PSALM 103:19)

"Not everyone who says to Me, 'Lord, Lord,' will enter the kingdom of heaven, but he who does the will of My Father who is in heaven will enter. (MATTHEW 7:21)

"I know the plans that I have for you," declares the LORD. "They are plans for peace and not disaster, plans to give you a future filled with hope."

(JEREMIAH 29:11 GOD'S WORD TRANSLATION)

The thief comes only to steal and kill and destroy; I came that they may have life, and have it abundantly.

(JOHN 10:10)

Now to him who is able to do immeasurably more than all we ask or imagine, according to his power that is at work within us,   (EPHESIANS 3:20 NIV)

And the peace of God, which surpasses all comprehension, will guard your hearts and your minds in Christ Jesus.

(PHILIPPIANS 4:7)

Though you have not seen him, you love him; and even though you do not see him now, you believe in him and are filled with an inexpressible and glorious joy

(1 PETER 1:8 NIV)

"Therefore everyone who confesses Me before men, I will also confess him before My Father who is in heaven.

(MATTHEW 10:32)

"As a father has compassion on his children, so the Lord has compassion on those who fear Him; for He knows how we are formed, He remembers that we are dust

(PSALM 103:13,14 NIV)

But from everlasting to everlasting the Lord's love is with those who fear Him..."   (PSALM 103:17 NIV).

"If we confess our sins, he is faithful and righteous to forgive us our sins and cleanse us from all unrighteousness"

(1 JOHN 1:9)

GROUP ACTIVITIES

1. Share your answers to questions 1–3. Pray for those who are struggling to submit to His Lordship. Encourage one another with your testimonies of God's grace.

2. Share your memory verses with each other. Talk about why you chose that verse to hide in your heart and what it means to you.

3. Pray together a prayer of commitment to submit to the Lordship of Jesus Christ in your lives.

3

A Great Salvation

When you were born again, you were no doubt told that now you no longer needed to fear hell because you had eternal life—you were going to live forever in Heaven with the Lord. Praise God for that! Death has been swallowed up in victory and no longer has the power to terrorize us (1 Cor. 15:54, 55)! We know that to leave the home of our physical body is to be at home instead with the Lord (2 Cor. 5:8). Jesus Himself has gone ahead to prepare a place for us to stay in the Father's own house (Jn. 14:2)! It's going to be awesome!

But we are not in Heaven yet, are we? Though we have been born again, we still have lives to live here on this earth. Are they to only be days of struggle in which we are comforted by the fact that one day we will finally be whisked away to peace and joy in the sweet by and by? Absolutely not! Eternal life began for you the moment you believed:

*Whoever believes in the Son **has** eternal life.* (JN. 3:36, 6:47)

It doesn't say that when you die you will have eternal life. No, it says that right here, right now in the present tense, you have eternal life. All that Jesus accomplished for you on the cross begins the moment you believe. Heaven is just the frosting on the cake!

WHAT DOES IT MEAN TO "BE SAVED"?

The New Testament was originally written in the Greek language, and understanding the nuances and depths of meaning of the words the writers used can often be very rewarding. The Greek word that is translated "save" is *sozo*, and it actually means "to save, deliver, protect, heal, preserve, do well, and be made whole." Those are all present tense realities, things God wants to do for you right now. Jesus' death on the cross delivers you, protects you, heals you, preserves you, makes your life go well, and makes you whole. His salvation touches not only your soul and spirit but every area of your life, starting the day you believe. You can begin living a heavenly life here on earth because you have received the Holy Spirit (Acts 2:38).

THE CROSS WAS ENOUGH!

The torture, death and resurrection of Jesus Christ provides for every need you have—spirit, soul and body—past, present and future.

> *His divine power has granted to us **everything pertaining to life and godliness**, through the true knowledge of Him who called us by His own glory and excellence.* (2 PET. 1:3)

Let's take a look at this great salvation He has purchased for you.

- Before you were born again, your iniquities separated you from your God; your sins hid His face from you, so that He did not hear (Is. 59:2). Your independence, rebellion and sin kept you apart from God, destroying the sweet fellowship with Him for which you were created. But Jesus came to change that!

*This is eternal life, **that they may know You**, the only true God, and Jesus Christ, whom You have sent.*   (JN. 17:3)

The essence of the eternal life that you have been given is that you can know God the Father and Jesus Christ the Son— now, currently, in the present tense. The Greek word used for "know" in this verse does not mean to simply perceive or understand something as fact or to merely be aware of a truth. This word means that you have a personal, experiential knowledge. It is the word used for the intimate "knowing" of a husband and wife. You can not only know *about* God but you can *know* Him—personally, intimately, meaningfully in your day to day life.

This new relationship with God is the foundation and the source of your new life. God is not a genie who just grants wishes, but a Father Who teaches, helps, guides, and gives out of His loving relationship with His children. It is as you get to know God better, listen to His voice, and receive His direction that you will be led into the abundant life you have been promised. As you are guided by what you hear from Him day by day, you will work out the glorious salvation you have received, for it is God who is at work in you, giving you both the desire and the ability to please Him (Phil. 2:12, 13).

You are loved, accepted and embraced by God. If Jesus had given us nothing else in our salvation, the ability to get to know our God personally would have been enough. But He has done so much more.

- Before you were born again, your heart was more deceitful than all else and desperately sick (Jer. 17:9). It was hard as stone because of your sin and separation from God. It was crooked, dishonest, weak and pitifully ill. You did not know God nor could you understand Him. You did not obey Him and you didn't want to. You rejected His ways and went astray. But the Lord said:

> *I will give you a new heart and put a new spirit within you; and I will remove the heart of stone from your flesh and give you a heart of flesh. I will put My Spirit within you and cause you to walk in My statutes, and you will be careful to observe My ordinances.*   (EZ. 36:26, 27)

Jesus has taken out that cold, darkened heart and replaced it with a new, soft heart that is filled with His Holy Spirit. Now you hunger after God, you enjoy sweet fellowship with Him, and you are happy to submit to Him in every way. You have peace and contentment within as you walk in holiness and obedience. The way of righteousness is not a burden you must take on but is the desire of your heart. Jesus removed the control sin held over you, giving you instead the power and passion to live a holy life. The compulsion toward sinful desires has been removed and you are free (1 Pet. 2:24)

- *He made Him who knew no sin to be sin on our behalf, so that we might become the righteousness of God in Him.*   (2 COR. 5:21)

Jesus not only removed your sinfulness; He gave you His own righteousness in its place. Not only was your slate wiped clean of all your sins; He replaced your history with the spotless record of His perfect Son. "God took the sinless Christ and poured into Him all your sins. Then, in exchange, He poured God's righteousness into you!" (2 Cor. 5:21 Living

Bible) He has wrapped you in a robe of righteousness like a bride arrays herself with beautiful jewels (Is. 61:10). You are clean on the inside, full of joy and peace. You are spotless in God's eyes—perfect, holy, righteous, and flawless.

- *"He took on our infirmities, and carried our diseases."* (MATT. 8:17)

By His wounds you were healed. (1 PET. 2:24)

Jesus Himself took on all your sickness, weakness, suffering, frailty and disease, and has given you full, vibrant, divine health. The very same Spirit that raised Christ from the dead and instantly healed all of the lacerations on His body from the whip and the thorns—that same Spirit now lives inside of you, empowering and revitalizing your body as well.

One of the names by which God revealed Himself to His people is *Jehovah Rapha*, meaning "I am the Lord that heals you." It is His nature to heal you and His desire that you walk in divine health. He wants you to go to Him first, in childlike faith, about any physical need you may have.

My sister-in-law was a nurse working in a doctor's office. One day when she tried to prepare a syringe, she didn't have the strength. A few days later, she wasn't able to hold onto a tray of instruments. As her weakness increased, she became more and more concerned. Extensive tests were run until the diagnosis was given: Lou Gehrig's disease. Her prognosis was grim, even with the best medical care available to her. Gradually her muscles deteriorated; she could no longer walk. Soon she might be unable to speak, eat, move or even breathe.

But Kathy believed God's promises that He was her Healer and that by the wounds Jesus bore, she would receive healing. Prayer chains brought her before the Lord daily. Other believers laid hands on her and believed with her. Finally, she attended a healing crusade with evangelist Benny Hinn. Her husband carried her to the balcony while an usher brought her wheelchair. The first night she returned to her hotel room with no change. The second night again brought no change. But Kathy was determined that she would not leave that place without her healing. The third day, as the crowd worshipped and the minister spoke, she felt the power of God come upon her. She stood up from her wheelchair and began to walk, her strength increasing with every step. She was healed!

A year later, she danced with her son at his wedding. It has now been more than 21 years and she is still healed! How can we not praise such a good God?

Your physical healing is so important to God that all three Persons of the Trinity have done their part to bring it to you. The Father has said, "I AM your Healer." The Son suffered torture in His body to purchase your healing. And the Spirit has taken up residence within your physical body where His life force radiates divine health to your every cell (Rom. 8:11). Physical healing is available for you!

• *Though He was rich, yet for your sake He became poor, so that you through His poverty might become rich.* (2 COR. 8:9)

Jesus has taken your poverty so that you can live in abundance. It is not His will for His children to lack the basic necessities of life (Ps. 37:25). The covenant blessings that are available to you if you will listen to His voice and obey Him include lending to others and not borrowing (Deut. 28:12). Everything that you put your hand to will be blessed

(Deut. 28:8). You will not lack but will have more than enough so that you can share with others (2 Cor. 8).

- *In everything by prayer and supplication, with thanksgiving, let your requests be made known to God; and the peace of God, which surpasses all understanding, will guard your hearts and minds through Christ Jesus* (PHIL. 4:6,7)

Jesus wants to take your fear, worry and anxiety and give you joy and peace to guard your heart. He cares about the things that you care about. If it is important to you, it is important to Him. He doesn't want you to carry the burden of worry, especially about things that you cannot control. He is much stronger than you and He wants to carry that burden for you, just because He loves you so much (1 Pet. 5:7). When you give your cares to Him, trusting His love to work things out according to His perfect will, your heart and mind will be flooded with a peace and calm no matter what the circumstances.

ONLY THE BEGINNING

These are only a taste of the multitude of blessings that are yours as a child of the King. As you continue to grow in the Lord, He will show you more and more about your new life. All these things are available to you by faith and obedience to His leading in your heart.

ADDITIONAL RESOURCES

- *Rise Up*—Michael Whate
- *The Basics in 21 Days*—Benjamin and Micah Joy Williams

YOUR *EXTRAORDINARY* LIFE

1. Carefully read through these verses:

"DEATH IS SWALLOWED UP in victory."

(1 CORINTHIANS 15:54)

We are of good courage, I say, and prefer rather to be absent from the body and to be at home with the Lord.

(2 CORINTHIANS 5:8)

My Father's house has many rooms; if that were not so, would I have told you that I am going there to prepare a place for you? (JOHN 14:2 NIV)

These verses are your promise that you no longer need to fear death. Because you have received Jesus as your Lord and Savior, you can have confidence that when you leave this life, you are merely stepping into another, better life. You will be leaving your earthly home and entering God's heavenly home that Jesus Himself has prepared for you!

Have you been afraid to die? Did you at least wonder what it would be like on the other side of death? Now that you have seen the Lord's promises to you in His Word, does that change the way you think of death and eternity? Do you have confidence that when you die, you will go home to the Father? Does that change anything about the way you live or think?

_____

_____

_____

_____

2. Write out for yourself all the meanings of the Greek word "sozo." Think about your life in light of all these promises. In what ways do you want to trust God to do all those things for you? For example, in what areas of your life do you need protection? Take time to talk with God about your needs and ask Him to meet them.

_____

_____

_____

_____

_____

3. *"Whoever believes in the Son **has** eternal life"* (Jn. 3:36, 6:47). What do you think it means for you to have eternal life right now?

_____

_____

_____

4. *"This is eternal life, that they may know You, the only true God, and Jesus Christ, whom You have sent"* (JOHN 17:3).

Think about what it might mean for you to experience a personal, meaningful relationship with the God Who created the Universe. What would it be like to really get to know Him as a close Friend, a Father, a Brother? How would it change the way you see yourself if you knew that the Master of the Universe was your best friend?

_____

_____

_____

_____

_____

5. Take a little time to really think about these verses:

> *I will give you a new heart and put a new spirit within you; and I will remove the heart of stone from your flesh and give you a heart of flesh. I will put My Spirit within you and **cause you to walk in My statutes, and you will be careful to observe My ordinances.*** (EZEKIEL 36:26, 27)

> *"He Himself bore our sins in His body on the cross, so that we might **die to sin and live to righteousness"***
> (1 PETER 2:24)

What do you think that means to you personally? What has God promised to do for you and in you? What kind of changes can you expect to see in your life because God has done these things for you?

----

6. Spend some time looking at these verses. Ask the Holy Spirit to show you what He wants to say to you through them.

> *"Repent, and each of you be baptized in the name of Jesus Christ for the forgiveness of your sins; and **you will receive the gift of the Holy Spirit**."* (ACTS 2:38)

> *Do you not know that you are a temple of God and that **the Spirit of God dwells in you**?* (1 CORINTHIANS 3:16)

> *But if the Spirit of Him who raised Jesus from the dead dwells in you, He who raised Christ Jesus from the dead*

will also give life to your mortal bodies through His Spirit who dwells in you.   (ROMANS 8:11)

"He took on our infirmities, and carried our diseases."

(MATTHEW 8:17)

By His wounds you were healed.   (1 PETER 2:24)

What promises is the Lord giving to you right now through these verses? How are you going to respond to what He is showing you?

_____

_____

_____

_____

_____

We will be looking at healing more as we explore how to "work out our salvation" (Philippians 2:12).

7. Take a look at these verses:

I have been young and now I am old,
  Yet I have not seen the righteous forsaken
  Or his descendants begging bread.

(PSALM 37:25)

My God will supply all your needs according to His riches in glory in Christ Jesus.   (PHILIPPIANS 4:19)

Seeing that His divine power has granted to us everything pertaining to life and godliness, through the true knowledge of Him who called us by His own glory and excellence.

(2 PETER 1:3)

And all these blessings shall come upon you and overtake you, if you obey the voice of the LORD your God...The LORD will command the blessing on you...in all that you undertake...The LORD will open to you his good treasury, the heavens, to give the rain to your land in its season and to bless all the work of your hands. And you shall lend to many nations, but you shall not borrow.

(DEUTERONOMY 28:2, 8, 12 ESV)

What do these verses promise you? What does the Lord want to say to you through His Word?

_____

_____

_____

_____

_____

The Bible actually spends more time on the topic of money and the right way to handle it than it does on prayer or even faith. We will return to this subject in a future chapter when we talk more about how to work out our salvation.

8. Carefully read these verses and think about what they say:

*In everything by prayer and supplication, with thanksgiving, let your requests be made known to God; and **the peace of God, which surpasses all understanding, will guard your hearts and minds** through Christ Jesus*

(PHILIPPIANS 4:6,7)

*[Cast] all your anxiety on Him, because **He cares for you**.*

(1 PETER 5:7)

*The things you have learned and received and heard and seen in me, practice these things, and **the God of peace will be with you**.* (PHILIPPIANS 4:9)

What do these verses say to you? What does God want you to talk to Him about? Why?

_____

_____

_____

_____

_____

9. Treasure God's word in your heart. Choose one of the verses you meditated on in the previous questions, or any verse from Chapter 3 that especially spoke to you. Write it down where you can see it often. Think about it throughout your day. Memorize it so that the truth becomes part of the way you think about yourself.

GROUP ACTIVITIES

1. Share your answers to questions 1–8. Answer any questions raised by anyone.

2. Share the verses that you memorized. Talk about why you chose that verse, what it means to you, and any way the Lord has used that verse to help you.

4

Water Baptism

It was amazing! They had seen with their own eyes the horror of the crucifixion and had taken His body themselves to the tomb for burial. Yet now Jesus was alive! For nearly six weeks the disciples had spent time with Him, receiving His final instructions before He returned to Heaven. How precious these moments were to them, and how they treasured every word He said, recognizing how important they were to Him. One of the very last things He said was, "Go and make disciples of all nations, baptizing them in the name of the Father and the Son and the Holy Spirit, teaching them to observe all that I commanded you, and lo, I am with you always, even to the end of the age" (Matt. 28:18-30). An important part of the message of the Gospel and making disciples was water baptism.

His disciples were careful to obey His command. When Peter finished preaching his first sermon in the book of Acts, he had convinced his audience that the Jesus Whom they had crucified was both Lord and Christ. They were pierced to the heart at the realization and cried out to him, "What shall we do?" They recognized that accepting Jesus as Lord required some kind of response from them. Peter answered, "Repent, and each of you be baptized in the Name of Jesus Christ for the forgiveness of your sins; and you will receive the gift of the Holy Spirit." Those who received his word were baptized; and that day about three thousand souls were added to the Kingdom (Acts 2:37-41).

Philip was another of the early disciples of Jesus. One day, the Holy Spirit directed Philip to go to a certain desert road. When he arrived, he found a court official from Ethiopia reading prophecies from the book of Isaiah. Philip explained to him that Isaiah was talking about Jesus and told him how he could be saved by believing in Him. As soon as the Ethiopian received the truth, he said, "Look! Water! What prevents me from being baptized?" He understood that believing in his heart called for a physical, visible response. So Philip and the official went down into the water and Philip baptized him (Acts 8:26-40).

WHat Does It mean?

The word "baptize" simply means to submerge, immerse or dip under. In Christian water baptism, you are briefly immersed under water and then brought back up. There are several layers of meaning to this ceremony. First, it beautifully illustrates the death, burial and resurrection of Christ. At the same time, it is an outward demonstration of what has happened to you in the new birth (Rom. 6:3,4, Col. 2:12). Your old man—that independent self that demanded its own way and thought it was the center of the universe—has died. What do you do with something that is dead? You bury it. And so baptism symbolically shows that your old self is dead and buried and no longer in control. As you are brought back up out of the water, it is the new you who is a child of God who comes forth, rising in newness of life.

In many countries and cultures of the world, even today, submitting to Christian water baptism takes great courage. Other religions recognize that it symbolizes the complete breaking away from old beliefs, laws and customs and the total embrace of Jesus as Lord. It is an act of obedience to your new Master, often your first act of obedience. I have heard it said that in some places they don't care if you say the words that define you as a believer. They will leave you alone in your delusion. But if you take the step of water baptism, you are sealing your fate and opening yourself to rejection, persecution and even death.

A sacrament, releasing Grace

While we may consider ourselves lucky to be able to be baptized without fear of consequences, perhaps that safety has lulled us into forgetting how powerful and important a step it is. Water baptism is one of the doorways that open up more of God's grace to us. The Church has historically considered water baptism to be a sacrament, which means it is a visible ceremony by which God confers His grace upon us. To understand the power involved, consider the sacrament of matrimony. Remember the words of Jesus concerning marriage, "What God has joined together, let no man put asunder" (Matt. 19:4-6)? Through the marriage ceremony, God supernaturally and mysteriously unites a man and women into one flesh (Mk. 10:8).

If we will have faith to believe it, water baptism can be a sacrament wherein God gives us the grace to die to sinful patterns and live in victory. I have personally known individuals who have gone under the waters of baptism as smokers and risen up free from the addiction. So you see, while it is a picture of your death and burial in Him, it can be much more than that, if you will believe. If you will embrace it in faith, God will use the opportunity of your baptism to cut the power of sinful habits out of your life and release you to a new level of holiness that you have not known before (1 Pet. 3:21, Rom. 6:4, Col. 2:11-14).

Repent and Be Baptized

Throughout the New Testament, believing in Christ for salvation and water baptism go together (Acts 2:41, Acts 8:26-39, Acts 9:18, Acts 10:47,48, Acts 16:13-15, Acts 16:16-34, Rom 6:1-7, Gal. 3:27, 1 Pet. 3:21). You have repented and received Jesus as your Lord and Savior; now it is time for you to be baptized in the Name of Jesus Christ. Find a believer or a group of believers who will baptize you immediately. It doesn't need to be an ordained minister; any believer who will join you in celebration and faith is qualified. Any source of water will do—a pond, lake, river, swimming pool, tub, or church baptistry—as long as it is big enough for you to be immersed in, it will be fine. There is no need to wait.

If any friends or family are there to observe your baptism, it is a great time to give a short testimony of the fact that you have received Jesus Christ as your Lord and Savior, and to talk about what He has done in you and for you.

As you stand in the water, the person doing the baptizing will say, "I baptize you in the Name of the Lord Jesus Christ, in the name of the Father, the Son and the Holy Spirit." He or she will gently tip you backwards, fulling immersing you, then lift you right back up.

Set your faith to believe for miracles of deliverance from sin and transformation as you go under the waters of baptism. Other people have experienced instantaneous freedom from sin patterns through water baptism. You can, too. Believe for it!

ADDITIONAL RESOURCES

• *Foundational Truths for Christian Living*—Derek Prince

PERSONAL APPLICATION

1. If you are not convinced that you should be baptized in water as soon as possible, read through all of the verses that show the connection between salvation and water baptism. Is there a reason why you should not or would not want to be baptized?

_____

_____

_____

2. Slowly and prayerfully read through this important Scripture passage about water baptism, taking the time to listen to the Holy Spirit within you to show you the wonderful promises it reveals:

> *Or do you not know that all of us who have been baptized into Christ Jesus have been baptized into His death? Therefore, we have been buried with Him through baptism into death, so that as Christ was raised from the dead through the glory of the Father, so we too might walk in newness of life. For if we have become united with Him in the likeness of His death, certainly we shall also be in the likeness of His resurrection, knowing this, that our old self was crucified with Him, in order that our body of sin might be done away with, so that we would no longer be slaves to sin; for he who has died is freed from sin.*

(ROMANS 6:4-7)

What does the Bible say happens in baptism, in your own words? What can you expect to happen to you (spiritually) when you are baptized?

_____

_____

_____

_____

_____

3. Is there a particular sinful habit that has persisted since your salvation? Would you like to be free of it? Will you allow it to be buried in the waters of baptism?

_____

_____

_____

_____

_____

4. Find a believer or group of believers who will baptize you. Prepare to say a few words about how God has changed you and what He means to you. (We call this, "giving your testimony.")

GROUP ACTIVITIES

1. Share answers to questions 1–3.

2. Hold a baptism service, ministering grace and celebrating new life.

5

A Light to Your Path

Have you ever visited a large cave or cavern and, once you were deep in the earth, had the guide turn out all the lights? Can you imagine how it would feel to try to explore that cave without any kind of lamp? You would creep along, an inch at a time, feeling your way carefully, always on the alert for unknown dangers. But with a light and a guide, you walk confidently along trails you have never walked before, peering over ledges and into deep pools that would be treacherous in the dark.

Or have you ever driven at night out west, far from city lights, perhaps climbing an unfamiliar mountain road? Now imagine that your car has no headlights, there are no street lights, and you are alone on the mountain in absolute darkness. How fast and how far do you think you will move forward?

You might feel like you are suddenly walking an unfamiliar path now that you have accepted Jesus into your life. You want to follow the right road but you can't see it yet. But don't worry—He has provided you with a light and a Guide to make your way clear.

A Lamp and a Guide

"Your word is a lamp to my feet and a light to my path"
(PS. 119:105).

"When the Spirit of truth comes, He will guide you into all truth"
(JN. 16:13)

God has given us the Bible as a lamp to light the way before us. We don't need to worry about taking a wrong path or stumbling into trouble unaware if we spend time getting to know what God has said to us through His Word. There we learn how He has related to His children throughout history. We discover all the wonderful promises He has made to us. And we learn how to live in a way that not only pleases Him but also brings joy and peace to our own lives. Getting to know the Scriptures is one of the very best ways to increase the power of grace in you.

But the most amazing thing about the Bible is that we have the Author with us Who can explain exactly what He meant and what it means to us as we read (2 Tim. 3:16)! We don't have to attempt to figure it out with our own minds. If we try, we are reverting back to that original temptation of independent living. Instead, we always come to the Word in a spirit of total dependence, knowing that we don't really know anything, that our attempts to dissect and decipher it only lead to fighting and divisions. Only the Author, the Spirit of Truth, can teach us and lead us into all truth (Jn. 14:26, Jn. 16:13).

"The Helper, the Holy Spirit, whom the Father will send in My name, He will teach you all things, and bring to your remembrance all that I said to you" (JN. 14:26).

41

Start with Matthew

If Holy Spirit is going to "bring to your remembrance all that [Jesus] has said to you," you first must hear what Jesus has to say. So begin today reading through the New Testament. Especially if you are a new believer who has never done so before, simply start at the beginning of Matthew and read straight through to Revelation. Before you begin, ask the Holy Spirit to speak to you through what you are reading, to open the eyes of your heart so you can get to know Jesus and see spiritual truth (Eph. 1:18). Do this every time you read the Scriptures. Never open your Bible without a humble dependence on the Holy Spirit to explain it to you.

So, begin in Matthew and read about the birth, life, death and resurrection of Jesus. (Family history was very important to the Jews so the first few verses of Matthew give Joseph's family tree. Don't worry—the story of Jesus' birth begins in verse 18.) Ask the Holy Spirit to use your imagination to help you see and experience what you are reading. Continue on through Mark, Luke and John, seeing many of the same events from different viewpoints and getting to know your Lord Jesus more and more.

Go on through the story of the new Church in the book of Acts, read the letters of church leaders to various fledgling congregations, until the final Revelation that came to John that reveals the ultimate triumph of Christ and His Bride, the Church. Don't stop to linger during this reading. Don't question or study or examine. Just absorb. Just let the Holy Spirit give you an overview of the richness of the life He will be leading you into. Just see Jesus as He was when He walked on earth and as He is now, seated in glory at the right hand of the Father. You should be able to read through the whole New Testament in a week or two.

There are many different versions of the Bible available today so it can be confusing to know which one to use. It is important to make sure you use an accurate translation so that what you are meditating on is truth and not a wrong interpretation of what God originally said. Translations which are very accurate and written in contemporary language include the New King James Bible, the New American Standard Bible Updated, the Modern English Version, and the King James Easy Read Bible. There are several excellent websites that host a variety of translations such as www.BibleHub.com and www.BibleGateway.com. Spend some time exploring the recommended translations on these sites before you buy so you get the one that you understand best.

Once you have read through the New Testament, you will want to continue reading through the whole Bible so you get a fuller picture of how God has been at work throughout history, intimately involved in the lives of individuals and overseeing the rise and fall of nations. Remember, this is still simply reading, seeing and absorbing under the guidance of the Holy Spirit.

There are many plans available for reading through the entire Bible in one year. Probably the simplest is to read three chapters each day and five chapters on Sunday. Many people like to read some Old Testament and some New Testament each day and there are many plans available to do that, including one on Bible Hub. There are resources that guide you through the Bible in chronological order, which in some cases is different than the biblical order. Choose a plan and stick with it for a year, then next year, try something different. But make regular Bible reading, overseen by the Holy Spirit, a part of your life, because through it the Lord will release more and more grace toward you.

Meditate, too

In addition to simply reading and getting a general understanding of the Scriptures, you will also want to meditate on specific verses, passages, chapters, books or subjects, as the Spirit guides you. Meditation is much more than merely reading and much deeper than simply studying with your mind.

> *"This book of the law shall not depart from your mouth, but you shall **meditate on it day and night**, so that you may be careful to do according to all that is written in it; for **then you will make your way prosperous, and then you will have success"***
> (JOSH. 1:8).

> *"How blessed is the man...whose delight is in the law of the LORD, and **in His law he meditates day and night**. He will be like a tree firmly planted by streams of water, which **yields its fruit** in its season and its leaf **does not wither**; and in **whatever he does, he prospers"*** (PS. 1:1-3)

What amazing promises God has given to those who will meditate on His Word and obey it: prosperity, success and enduring fruit! To receive the full benefits of the Scriptures, we must meditate on them, allowing them to become part of who we are.

So how does meditation differ from reading or studying? Both the Greek (New Testament) and Hebrew (Old Testament) words that are translated as a form of "meditate" include reading and studying, but those are only a small part of it. Meditation also involves talking, singing, roaring, pondering, reflecting, praying, expressing devotion, worshiping, and imagining. It is related to the word that would describe a cow chewing her cud—bringing something back up over and over to "digest" it again and again until you have received all the good from it you can and it has become flesh in you.

HOW TO MEDITATE

To help you develop the practice of meditation on Scripture, here is the simple plan that I follow. (Don't worry if you don't understand some of the suggestions. We will be learning more about them in future chapters.)

1. **Write:** I copy the verse by hand onto a piece of paper or 3X5 card (Deut. 17:18) and keep it with me to meditate on, memorize and mutter throughout the day(s). I also record this verse in my meditation journal (which can be written, typed or verbally recorded).

2. **Quiet Down:** I become still in God's presence, loving Him through soft soaking music (2 Kings 3:15, 16), praying in tongues (1 Cor. 14:14), or putting a smile on my face and picturing Jesus with me (Acts 2:25). I tune to His flowing thoughts, pictures and emotions (Jn. 7:37-39).

3. **Reason:** I reason together with God (Isa. 1:18), meaning the Spirit guides my reasoning process through flow. "Lord, what do You want to show me about any of the following: the context of the verse, the Hebrew/Greek definitions of the key words in the verse, any cultural understandings?" (See the Suggested Resources at the end for tools that will help you with these.)

4. **Speak & Imagine:** I ponder the Scripture, speaking it to myself softy over and over again until I can say it with my eyes closed. As I repeat the Scripture, I allow myself to see its truth with the eyes of my heart. I note what the picture is in my mind's eye as I repeat the Scripture.

5. **Feel:** God's Heart: While seeing the above picture, I ask, "Lord, what does this Scripture reveal about Your heart toward me?" I feel His heart and write what I sense.

6. **Hear:** God's *Rhema*: I put myself in the picture of this Scripture in my mind. I ask, "Lord, what are You speaking to me through this Scripture?" I tune to flowing thoughts and flowing pictures (God's voice and vision) and I record this dialogue in my two-way journaling.

7. **Act:** I accept this revelation, repenting of any sin that is opposite of it and roaring at any obstacle that stands in the way of implementing it. I then speak it forth and act on it.

The Holy Spirit guides this process, leading to more or less emphasis on any of the various steps, according to God's wishes for the present moment and the personal needs we have. We remain dependent upon Him throughout. For example, I may need more or less time to quiet myself in His presence, or more or less time in Spirit-led "reasoning," or doing two-way journaling about it, or roaring at the enemy to get his lies out of my head and his hands off my life. I allow the flow of the Holy Spirit to guide me through the steps of this meditation process.

THE RESULTS OF MEDITATION

When you start spending time meditating on God's Word, you will love it! There is nothing like the excitement of having verses leap off the page and into your heart as the Spirit illuminates them to you. Your heart burns within you as revelation grips you and you actually sense the work of the Spirit changing you into His likeness (Lk. 24:32, 2 Cor. 3:18). You will become addicted to that feeling and seek it as often as possible.

As you do your daily Bible reading, the Lord will sometimes focus your attention on a specific verse or passage that He wants you to look at more deeply. When He does that, obey His leading and spend time meditating until you have received all He has for you from those words.

Sometimes you will have a specific need in your life, such as for physical healing or victory over a specific sin pattern. Take those opportunities to do topical meditations, searching out everything the Bible says about the subject and meditating on each passage until it becomes flesh in you.

Perhaps as you read through this or other spiritual books, a verse that is quoted will draw your attention. Take the time to meditate on those verses because the Spirit wants to tell you something personal and special through them.

Transformed While We Look

The most exciting and important result of meditating on the Scriptures is the transformation we see in our lives as a result of time spent allowing the Holy Spirit to reveal Jesus to us. We have the promise that as we look at the glory of the Lord, we are transformed into the same image (2 Cor. 3:18). So spend time pondering, reflecting and imagining what the Bible says. Ask the Lord to give you a Spirit of wisdom and revelation in your knowledge of Him and to open the eyes of your heart so that you may know the hope of His calling, the riches of the glory of His inheritance in you, and the surpassing greatness of His power toward you (Eph. 1:17,18). God has chosen you to be conformed to the image of His Son (Rom. 8:29). That is your great destiny.

ADDITIONAL RESOURCES

- Free gift: 7 Step Meditation bookmark at http://www. cwgministries.org/sites/default/files/files/7-Step-Meditation-Bookmark.pdf
- We recommend you download the free Bible software e-Sword (www.e-sword.net). It has no cost training videos and several translations to get you started in meditating on the Bible. The two Bible translations I like best are the New American Standard Bible and the New King James Version because they are so accurate.
- *Hearing God Through Biblical Meditation*—Mark and Patti Virkler

PERSONAL APPLICATION

1. Slowly and carefully read through the verses below which were used in this chapter. Ask the Lord to give you a Spirit of wisdom and revelation and to open the eyes of your heart to see whatever He wants to show you through them.

   "Your word is a lamp to my feet and a light to my path"
                                                      (PS. 119:105).

   "When the Spirit of truth comes, He will guide you into all truth"   (JN. 16:13)

   "The Helper, the Holy Spirit, whom the Father will send in My name, He will teach you all things, and bring to your remembrance all that I said to you"   (JN. 14:26).

   "This book of the law shall not depart from your mouth, but you shall meditate on it day and night, so that you may be careful to do according to all that is written in it;

for then you will make your way prosperous, and then you will have success" (JOSH. 1:8).

"How blessed is the man...whose delight is in the law of the LORD, and in His law he meditates day and night. He will be like a tree firmly planted by streams of water, which yields its fruit in its season and its leaf does not wither; and in whatever he does, he prospers" (PS. 1:1-3)

But we all, with unveiled face, beholding as in a mirror the glory of the Lord, are being transformed into the same image from glory to glory... (2 CORINTHIANS 3:18)

[I pray] that the God of our Lord Jesus Christ, the Father of glory, may give to you a spirit of wisdom and of revelation in the knowledge of Him. I pray that the eyes of your heart may be enlightened, so that you will know what is the hope of His calling, what are the riches of the glory of His inheritance in the saints, and what is the surpassing greatness of His power toward us who believe. These are in accordance with the working of the strength of His might.... (EPHESIAN 1:17, 18)

For those whom He foreknew, He also predestined to become conformed to the image of His Son, so that He would be the firstborn among many brethren; (ROMANS 8:29)

What is God saying to you through these verses? What promises are especially meaningful to you, and what do they mean to you personally? Record what the Lord shows you through the Scriptures so you can come back and be blessed when you read it again.

_____

_____

_____

2. Choose one of the verses you have read so far in this book to really meditate on, using the pattern given in Chapter 5 as much as you are able.

GROUP ACTIVITIES

1. Share your answers to the questions, encouraging and supporting each other in your growth in the Lord.

6

The Baptism in the Holy Spirit

It had been three long days since Jesus was crucified. His closest followers huddled together, hiding behind locked doors, afraid that those who had killed Jesus would soon be coming for them as well. They were trying to hold onto their faith but it was hard. They just couldn't believe that He was really gone. All their expectations for the future—all their plans for change—all gone, along with their hoped-for Messiah.

Sure, a couple of women from the group had come running in earlier claiming that His tomb was open and empty. They even talked about seeing a couple of angels there who said that Jesus had been raised from the dead. But really—that was just nonsense.

But then, two of the men returned unexpectedly. They had been heading home to nearby Emmaus, as discouraged as the rest of the disciples. But now they were excited! They said that the women were right, that Jesus had risen and that they had seen Him, too!

Everyone began talking at once. Could it be true? Was He really the Messiah as they had hoped and believed? Was He really alive again? How could that be possible? They had seen His horrible death. They had watched His broken body taken down from the cross and buried in Joseph's tomb. They had seen the guard that Pilate had posted after sealing the grave. It must be a mistake. But what if it wasn't? What if Jesus really has been raised like He promised? What if He really is alive?

Suddenly He was standing there in the room with them! At least, it looked like Him. And when He spoke, it sounded like Him. But maybe it was His ghost! He showed them the wounds on His hands and feet and ate a bit of broiled fish to convince them that He was real, He was Jesus, and He was alive.

Their fear turned to joy as He said, "Peace be with you!" Then He breathed on them and said, "Receive the Holy Spirit." He went on to explain the prophecies about Himself and His death and resurrection, then gave them instructions to go out and tell everyone what they had seen and heard. "But," He said, "stay in the city until you have been clothed with power from on high. Wait for the gift my Father promised. In a few days you will be baptized with the Holy Spirit! Then you will have the power to be my witnesses" (Matt. 27, 28; Luke 24; John 20; Acts 1). So they stayed in Jerusalem as He had charged them to.

"[And] when the day of Pentecost had come, they were all together in one place. And suddenly there came from heaven a noise like a violent rushing wind, and it filled the whole house where they were sitting. And there appeared to them tongues as of fire distributing themselves, and they rested on each one of them. And they were all filled with the Holy Spirit and began to speak with other tongues, as the Spirit was giving them utterance" (ACTS 2:1-4).

The promised Gift had come!

THE PROMISE IS FOR YOU!

Did you notice that when Jesus appeared to His disciples, He breathed on them and said, "Receive the Holy Spirit"? Just like you when you were born again, those early followers also were born of the Spirit. The Holy Spirit was joined to their spirits just as He was joined to yours when you accepted Jesus as Lord (1 Cor. 6:17, Jn. 20:22). They became children of God!

But Jesus wanted to give them more of His Spirit. The Spirit had come into them but He wanted to fill them to overflowing and have the Spirit rest upon them as well. He wanted them to be immersed in His Spirit. Just as they had been eye witnesses of Jesus' life, His teaching, His miracles, His death and His resurrection (Lk. 24:48), the baptism with the Holy Spirit would enable them to continue to be eye witnesses of what Jesus would continue to do in Jerusalem, Judea, Samaria and even to the uttermost parts of the earth (Acts 1:8). They would be empowered to see what Jesus was doing and tell others, because the Holy Spirit had come upon them.

Jesus wants to do the same for you. You have already had the Holy Spirit joined to your spirit when you accepted Jesus as Lord (1 Cor. 6:17; Jn. 20:22). Next He wants to fill you to overflowing, and even rest upon you (Acts 2:1-4), empowering you not only to live a holy life but to live a life of power. Just as there is a difference between receiving a glass of water and doing a cannonball into the deep end of a swimming pool, so there is a difference between receiving the Holy Spirit at salvation and being immersed in the Holy Spirit through baptism. Jesus promises that you will be "clothed with power from on high" when the Holy Spirit comes upon you (Luke 24:49)! You will be empowered to see and hear what Jesus is doing right now and be a witness for Him in your world.

The baptism in the Holy Spirit is a gift from the Father (Acts 1:4), so there is nothing you have to do to earn it or work up to it. All you have to do is tell Him that you want to receive the gift that He has promised you.

Early Church Patterns

Here are some passages that talk about various people in the early Church receiving the baptism in the Holy Spirit:

And they were all filled with the Holy Spirit and began to speak with other tongues, as the Spirit was giving them utterance. (ACTS 2:4)

While Peter was still speaking these words, the Holy Spirit fell on all who heard his message. All the circumcised believers who had accompanied Peter were amazed that the gift of the Holy Spirit had been poured out even on the Gentiles. For they heard them speaking in tongues and exalting God.

(ACTS 10:44-46)

When they heard this, they were baptized in the name of the Lord Jesus. And when Paul had laid his hands upon them, the Holy Spirit came on them, and they began speaking with tongues and prophesying. (ACTS 19:5,6)

Did you notice that speaking in tongues, or speaking in languages they had not learned, is recorded as accompanying the baptism in the Holy Spirit? In fact, in Acts 10 it appears that speaking in tongues was the proof to the others present that the believers had actually received the gift of the Holy Spirit. So when you receive the gift of the baptism in the Holy Spirit, you, too, can expect to begin to speak in tongues.

But What's It For?

Why would you want to speak in a language that you have not learned and don't even understand? The Bible gives us several benefits of speaking in tongues. On the day of Pentecost (Acts 2), at least some of the disciples were speaking of the mighty deeds of God in languages which were recognizable to people from other nations (Acts 2:5-12), so God used tongues to help them evangelize the lost. To other people who heard them, they sounded as if they were drunk (Acts 2:13), so it is possible that some of them were speaking not in languages of men but of angels (1 Cor. 13:1). We don't get to choose what language we speak; it is the Spirit Who gives us the pronunciation (Acts 2:4).

It is easy for us to understand why God might give us the ability to tell other people who speak a different language about Him. But why would God give us the ability to speak in the language of angels? Why would we even speak in other human languages if there was no one around to understand? In fact, we probably wouldn't know if what we were speaking was a language of men or angels, since we have never heard all the 6,500 languages spoken around the world. Why should we speak what sounds like gibberish to us?

Like the disciples in Acts 2, when you speak in tongues you may be talking about the wonderful things God has done. Or your spirit may be praying (1 Cor. 14:14), giving thanks (1 Cor. 14:17), or speaking mysteries to God (1 Cor. 14:2). Even though you don't understand what you are saying, you are edifying or building yourself up in the Spirit, growing in wisdom, strength, courage and holiness (1 Cor. 14:4). It is so important that the Apostle Paul declared that he spoke in tongues more than all the people in the Corinthian church (1 Cor. 14:18) and that he wished that everyone would speak in tongues (1 Cor. 14:5)!

We might not understand speaking in tongues and think it is a strange thing to do, but we must never scorn or reject it for it was God's idea and is a gift from Him. Who are we to think we know better than God what is a good gift? It is not the only spiritual gift that we earnestly desire, but it is the initial one that we receive when we are baptized in the Holy Spirit.

Receive it now

So when you tell God you are ready to receive His empowering gift of the Holy Spirit, you are saying that you want to speak in tongues, too, because that is what He wants you to do. If you are ready to be clothed with power from on high and you want everything the Father has promised you, you can pray a simple prayer right now and receive:

> *Father, thank You that You have promised to give me the gift of the baptism in the Holy Spirit. Father God, I want to receive that gift. I want to be clothed with power from on high so that I can be a witness for You in my world. Holy Spirit, here I am. I offer myself fully to You. Fall upon me. Fill me and overwhelm me. Immerse me in Your love, Your grace, and Your power. Thank You, my Father, for Your wonderful gift. I receive it now.*

You might immediately begin speaking words that your mind is not thinking up. You may sense your tongue wanting to move and pronounce syllables that have not been directed by your mind. Many people have this experience and if you will release it in faith, just allowing your mouth to speak whatever it wants to, you will begin speaking in tongues.

However, some people do not feel that urge to speak and they wonder if they have actually received the gift of the Holy Spirit. If that is you, I want to assure you that you have! God has promised it and He doesn't lie. If you have asked in faith, God has given you the baptism in the Holy Spirit and the ability to speak in tongues. Speaking in tongues is a good gift given by a good God to build up your spirit. He would not give such an important gift to some people and withhold it from others. You can speak in tongues with just a little bit of instruction (and faith).

HOW to release Languages from the Spirit

To receive the gift of speaking in tongues, you must yield your vocal cords to the flow of the Holy Spirit. Begin by fixing your eyes and heart on the Lord Jesus Christ, worshipping before His throne. Speak out loud, words of praise, thanksgiving and love. After a few minutes of heartfelt worship from your spirit, deliberately yield control over what you are saying to the Holy Spirit and allow syllables to continue to flow out. Keep speaking but don't think about or plan what you are going to say. Simply keep focusing on your Lord and all He means to you and allow whatever sounds to come out that your vocal cords and tongue want to form. You choose to speak, but you choose to not control the formation of the syllables (Acts 2:4). You choose to believe that the River of the Holy Spirit which flows within you is guiding your pronunciation. You trust God to arrange those sounds into a language that pleases Him, and you will find yourself speaking in tongues.

Don't delay! This gift is for you today. Begin now to spend time praying in tongues, glorifying God, speaking mysteries to Him, and building up your spirit. Take time every day to enjoy this unique gift that the Father designed just for you. The more often you offer yourself to Him in this way, the more your faith will grow and the greater the flow of words will be.

If you begin with just a few sounds or phrases, just keep offering them back to God as a sacrifice of faith. Ask Him to release more of Himself in you and through you, then by faith offer more words back to Him. Your language will grow as your faith increases and your spirit becomes stronger. It will be a lovely cycle of growth in grace as you offer more and receive more and your faith increases, so you offer more and receive more, and on and on!

ADDITIONAL RESOURCES

- *How to Receive the Baptism in the Holy Spirit* —Mark and Patti Virkler
- *How to Speak in Tongues* CD/DVD set—Mark Virkler
- *How Holy Spirit Baptism Unlocks the Supernatural* —Charity Kayembe (https://www.youtube.com/ watch?v=JPYGC1lS1ts)
- *Foundational Truths for Christian Living*—Derek Prince
- *Baptized in the Spirit*—Randy Clark

PERSONAL APPLICATION

1. Ask the Holy Spirit to reveal to you personally what He wants you to see today through the following verses:

   *"**You will receive power** when the Holy Spirit has come upon you; and **you shall be My witnesses** both in Jerusalem, and in all Judea and Samaria, and even to the remotest part of the earth."* (ACTS 1:8)

*"And behold, I am sending forth the promise of My Father upon you; but you are to stay in the city until **you are clothed with power** from on high."* (LUKE 24:49)

---

2. Slowly read the account of the very first people who received the baptism in the Holy Spirit in Acts 2:1-13. Meditate on the passage, using the eyes of your heart to see what the scene might have been like. Ask the Holy Spirit to speak to you through the Scriptures.

   Describe the scene in your own words, as if you were there in the house with the disciples or in the crowd that gathered.

   ---

3. What was the purpose of speaking in other tongues on the day of Pentecost? Do you believe God might do the same thing today? Why or why not? If He might, under what circumstances do you think it might happen? Are you open to the Lord using you in this way?

   ---

4. What all does the following verse teach about the languages that we speak?

    If I speak with the tongues of men and of angels, but do not have love, I have become a noisy gong or a clanging cymbal.
    (1 CORINTHIANS 13:1)

    _____
    _____
    _____

5. What do these verses say happens when you speak in tongues?

    For if I pray in a tongue, my spirit prays....
    (1 CORINTHIANS 14:14)

    One who speaks in a tongue edifies himself....
    (1 CORINTHIANS 14:4)

    But you, beloved, building yourselves up on your most holy faith, praying in the Holy Spirit, keep yourselves in the love of God...
    (JUDE 20, 21)

    What does that mean to you personally?

    _____
    _____
    _____
    _____
    _____

6. The following passage is giving instructions for the proper way to express the gift of tongues in a church service:

    Therefore, let one who speaks in a tongue pray that he may interpret. For if I pray in a tongue, my spirit prays, but my mind is unfruitful. What is the outcome then? I will pray with the spirit and I will pray with the mind also; I will sing with the spirit and I will sing with the mind also. Otherwise if you bless in the spirit only, how will the one who fills the place of the ungifted say the "Amen" at your giving of thanks, since he does not know what you are saying? For you are giving thanks well enough, but the other person is not edified. (1 CORINTHIANS 14:13-17)

First, what should a person do who wants to speak in tongues in public do? Why?

_____

_____

What is the person who is speaking in tongues saying or doing?

_____

_____

Are you open to the Lord using you in this way?

_____

_____

7. *For one who speaks in a tongue does not speak to men but to God; for no one understands, but in his spirit he speaks mysteries.* (1 Corinthians 14:2)

What does this verse say about speaking in tongues? Is this something you are open to doing?

_____

_____

_____

8. Had you heard of speaking in tongues before reading this chapter? What did you know or believe about it previously? Has that belief changed at all as a result of the Scriptures you have meditated on? What is your current belief about speaking in tongues?

_____

_____

_____

_____

_____

9. Did you pray as directed at the end of the chapter? Did you receive the gift of the Holy Spirit? Did you begin to speak in tongues? If not, will you earnestly desire and pursue all that God has for you?

_____

_____

_____

_____

GROUP ACTIVITIES

1. Discuss your answers to all the questions.

2. Pray for anyone who desires the baptism in the Holy Spirit with the gift of speaking in tongues, giving instruction and encouragement until all who desire, receive.

7

The Lord's Supper

It was their last evening together. Even now, His enemies were conspiring—drawing nearer by the hour. It was hard to think about leaving His dear friends, knowing how frightened and confused they would be, how much they would suffer because of their loyalty to Him. Jesus looked around the table and thought about all that He still wanted to say to them, but time was growing short. This was the last meal they would share together in this life. Tomorrow He would fulfill His reason for coming to the world. He had known from the beginning what it would mean, but it was still difficult to contemplate. And His disciples didn't really understand even now.

How could He prepare them? What could He say that would help them through the dark days before them? How could He make them understand that His sacrifice was necessary and for their benefit?

Reaching out, Jesus took some bread, and after a blessing, He broke it and gave it to the disciples. "Take and eat it," He said. "This is My body which is given for you. Do this in remembrance of Me." Then He took a cup, gave thanks, and passed it around so that all His disciples had a drink from it. "This is My blood of the new covenant, which is poured out for many for forgiveness of sins. Do this, whenever you drink it, in remembrance of Me."

He knew they would understand what He was saying to them. They were people of the Covenant. They understood what the covenant relationship meant: that both partners in the agreement were committing everything they had and everything they were to the other person. A covenant was the strongest contract in their culture, requiring that both sides put aside their own interests and give themselves to the welfare of the other. And a covenant required the shedding of blood.

The bread and the fruit of the vine would become the covenant meal and a perpetual reminder to them that on this day they entered into a new covenant with their God. With this understanding and the Presence of the Holy Spirit He would send to them, Jesus was confident that His dear friends would be strong enough to face whatever was ahead of them. (See Matthew 26:26-29, Mark 14:22-25, Luke 22:14-20, and 1 Corinthians 11:23-25.)

"THIS IS MY BLOOD OF THE COVENANT"

The power of the blood covenant has been lost to us today but the disciples would have immediately understood what Jesus was offering them. If you and I were neighbors in ancient Israel, we might have decided to enter into a blood covenant with each other. We would have sacrificed one or more animals and made promises to each other. I might have said, "I want you to know that I have your back. If anyone attacks you or your home or family, it's as if they attacked me. I will be there fighting by your side along with my family and my servants. And if something happens to your crops or your herds so you don't have enough food, as long as I have anything in my storehouse, you don't need to worry about going hungry. Just let me know what you need and it's yours. Everything I have is at your disposal." And you would make similar promises to me. We might make a small cut in our palms then clasp hands so that our blood ran together, signifying that we are now "blood brothers." And we would eat a covenant meal together as a seal of our agreement.

That is what Jesus was symbolically showing His disciples when He said that what they were drinking was the blood of the new covenant. He was giving them the opportunity to enter into a reciprocal relationship with God in which everything God possesses would be available to meet any need they might have. Never would they face any lack because they have a covenant partner Who has unlimited resources, and what belongs to their Partner is completely at their disposal. By entering into covenant, God had given them a blank check, the key to His storehouses, total access to all that He has and all that He is.

But because this was a covenant with God Almighty, He was offering to meet more than just their material needs. All previous covenants had been sealed by the shedding of the blood of animals (Gen. 15:9,10; Heb. 9:18,19). But this covenant was sealed by the shedding of the blood of the Son of God Himself, so it was able to meet the greatest need we had: forgiveness of our sins and restoration of relationship with our God (Matt. 26:28; Heb. 9:12-15, 28).

Jesus' death established the new covenant between God and man. His blood was poured out to wash away all of our sins. And every time we take the Lord's Supper, we are to remember what He has done. Paul warns us to examine ourselves as we take the bread and the cup (1 Cor. 11:27,28). So as we drink, we remember our Savior's great sacrifice for us, how He poured out

His precious blood and His very life to cleanse us from all sins, and we respond with deep gratitude and worship. We ask the Holy Spirit to reveal anything within us that is not pleasing to Him and anything we are holding back from Him. We confess our sin and repent, returning Him to His rightful place as Lord of our lives.

A covenant is between two parties, and both sides make the same total commitment to give themselves away to the other. We not only receive all that God has and is when we enter into this covenant, we also give to Him all that we have and all that we are to use in any way He desires. Clearly, we get the better deal in this relationship! But God Himself has extended the invitation to enter into covenant with Him, even knowing how weak and needy we are. When we drink the Lord's Supper, it is a reminder to us of His Lordship and a chance to once more recommit ourselves totally to Him.

"THIS IS MY BODY"

> *And when He had taken some bread and given thanks, He broke it and gave it to them, saying, "This is My body which is given for you; do this in remembrance of Me."* (LUKE 22:19)

There are two elements to the Lord's Supper, which some people call the Lord's Table, Communion, Holy Communion or the Eucharist. We have talked about the drink, which is often referred to as wine, and that is what some churches use. The Bible simply says it is "fruit of the vine," so other churches prefer to use grape juice.

Some churches pass around a loaf of bread and worshippers break off a piece to eat. Other churches pre-cut the bread into cubes. Some churches use unleavened bread and others use special wafers. The point is that it doesn't matter what elements you use; what is important is that as often as we eat the bread and drink from the cup, we proclaim the Lord's death (1 Cor. 11:26). It is our focus and our faith that make the covenant meal different from simply sharing a loaf of bread and glass of wine.

We have seen that when we drink we are reminded of the blood of Christ that was poured out for the forgiveness of our sins, and by faith we receive cleansing for any transgression that we have allowed into our lives. In the same way, we eat the bread in remembrance of Jesus' body that was given and broken for us. If the shedding of His blood washed away our sins, what did the sacrifice of His body do for us? What do we remember when we eat the bread?

Jesus endured terrible torture even before the agony of the crucifixion. When Pilate could find no guilt in Jesus but the crowds still demanded that he crucify Him, Pilate commanded Him to be scourged—lashed—whipped—flogged. Then the soldiers twisted together a crown of thorns and shoved it on His head and beat him on the head with a reed. He endured that abuse because those wounds were to bring us healing (Is. 53:5, 1 Pet. 2:24). He allowed His body to be broken so that ours would be healed.

So as you take the bread into your hand at the Lord's Table, do it in remembrance of Him. Don't let His suffering be in vain but receive the healing He purchased for you at such great cost. Just as you have believed in the power of His blood to wash away your sins, believe also in the power of His wounds to heal your diseases (Ps. 103:3). Proclaim the power of the Lord's death until He returns by walking in all the blessings He gave His life to give to you (Is. 53:4-6).

proclaim the Lord's Death

The cross, the Lord's death, is the focal point of Scripture, and throughout the Old and New Testaments we are given glimpses into all that He accomplished for us. The cross was a point of divine exchange, where Jesus took all our sins, weaknesses, and needs on Himself and gave us everything He has and is in return. Meditate on these blessings Jesus purchased for you through His death.

1. **Spiritual intimacy with God**—*They may be one, just as We are one* (Jn. 17:22).

2. **A healed heart**—*A new heart and a new spirit I give you* (Ezek. 36:26).

3. **Adorned with Christ's righteousness**—*We might become the righteousness of God in Him* (2 Cor. 5:21).

4. **Power over sin**—*He Himself bore our sins in His body on the cross, so that we might die to sin and live to righteousness* (1 Pet. 2:24).

5. **Divine glory**—*The glory which You have given Me I have given to them* (Jn. 17:22).

6. **The Holy Spirit**—*We receive the promise of the Spirit through faith* (Gal. 3:13-14).

7. **Physical healing**—*By His wounds you were healed* (1 Pet. 2:24).

8. **Financial prosperity**—*You through His poverty might become rich* (2 Cor. 8:9)

9. **Hope**—*Christ in you, the hope of glory* (Col. 1:27).

10. **Peace**—*In everything by prayer and supplication, with thanksgiving, let your requests be made known to God; and the peace of God, which surpasses all understanding, will guard your hearts and minds through Christ Jesus* (Phil. 4:6,7)

11. **A family**—*He predestined us to adoption as sons through Jesus Christ to Himself* (Eph. 1:5).

12. **Eternal life**—*The gift of God is eternal life through Jesus Christ our Lord* (Rom. 6:23).

When you take the Lord's Supper, you are proclaiming each of these truths about what the Lord's death accomplished for you. Reflect on them as you participate in Communion. See that they are true because of Christ's sacrifice. Receive them by faith in a deeper way each time you receive the bread and juice. If you have any need in your life, remember that you have a covenant Partner Who has already promised to meet those needs. As you eat and drink, let your faith be renewed, make your requests to God, and let His peace fill your heart and mind.

ONE LOAF, ONE BODY

Yet there is another mystery in the sharing of the bread. Paul tells us that "since there is one bread, we who are many are one body; for we partake of the one bread" (1 Cor. 10:17). We, the Church, are Christ's body, and individually members of it (1 Cor. 12:27). In the sharing of the loaf, here is another work of grace that the Lord wants to do in us: uniting us in spirit, stirring us up in love, making us as believers into one Body. Just as there is one loaf, even when it has been divided up among many people, there is one Spirit Who has joined Himself with the many believers who make up the Church. We have one Lord and one faith, one God and Father of all; there is one body and one Spirit. Therefore, let us walk with humility, gentleness, patience and love, making every effort to keep the unity of the Spirit in the bond of peace (Eph. 4:1-6). Taking the Lord's Supper together in faith can strengthen those bonds and establish relationships in meaningful and spiritual ways.

AS OFten as you eat...

The Lord's Supper is regarded as another sacrament of the Church—an outward ceremony in which the Lord imparts grace to His people. There is the grace of forgiveness of sins as we remember the blood of Jesus. There is the grace of healing when we remember His broken body. There is the grace of knowing that God has chosen to covenant with us to provide all our needs, both spiritual and physical (2 Pet. 1:3, Phil 4:19). There is the grace of all the blessings given through the divine exchange. And there is the grace of being part of a Body, no longer walking alone but a member of the royal priesthood, the holy nation, the Church of Jesus Christ (1 Pet. 2:9).

Paul exhorts us to remember Christ's death every time we eat bread and drink the fruit of the vine (1 Cor. 11:23-26). Some churches offer Communion in their services just a few times a year; others offer it every day to those who will come. But there is nothing in Scripture that says only an ordained minister can bless the elements and remember the Lord's death and receive the grace that is offered through the Lord's Supper.

Whenever you meet with fellow believers, you can share the bread and the cup and by faith receive whatever you need. In fact, there is no reason you cannot remember His sacrifice every time you eat and drink, even if there is no one else with you. You are still a member of the Body and a partner in the covenant, and His grace is available to you every day.

PERSONAL APPLICATION

1. Slowly and prayerfully read the following passage, asking the Holy Spirit to open your mind and heart to what He wants to say to you through it. Record what He says.

    He did not enter by means of the blood of goats and calves; but he entered the Most Holy Place once for all by his own blood, thus obtaining eternal redemption. The blood of goats and bulls and the ashes of a heifer sprinkled on those who are ceremonially unclean sanctify them so that they are outwardly clean. How much more, then, will the blood of Christ, who through the eternal Spirit offered himself unblemished to God, cleanse our consciences from acts that lead to death, so that we may serve the living God!

    For this reason Christ is the mediator of a new covenant, that those who are called may receive the promised eternal inheritance—now that he has died as a ransom to set them free from the sins committed under the first covenant...so Christ was sacrificed once to take away the sins of many;
    (HEBREWS 9:12-15, 28 NIV)

    _____

    _____

    _____

    _____

    _____

2. What does it mean to you personally to have entered into a blood covenant with the Almighty God?

    _____

    _____

    _____

3. What do these verses tell us about the reason and results of Jesus' allowing His body to be broken for you? Make your answer personal—what did He do for you?

    > *But He was pierced through for our transgressions,*
    >   *He was crushed for our iniquities;*
    > *The chastening for our well-being fell upon Him,*
    >   *And by His scourging we are healed.*   (ISAIAH 53:5)

    > *He Himself bore our sins in His body on the cross, so that we might die to sin and live to righteousness; for by His wounds you were healed.*   (1 PETER 2:24)

    > *Bless the LORD, O my soul,*
    >   *And forget none of His benefits;*
    > *Who pardons all your iniquities,*
    >   *Who heals all your diseases;*   (PSALM 103:2,3)

    _____

    _____

    _____

    _____

4. How can you "remember the Lord's death until He comes" with the bread and cup of the Lord's Table?

    _____

    _____

    _____

GROUP ACTIVITIES

1. Share your answers to the questions, discussing anything of special interest to the members of the group.

2. Share the Lord's Table together, in faith receiving all the gifts of grace that are available to you.

8

Conversations with Your Friend

Their enemies were coming and God would not be protecting them. The prophet Habakkuk had been shown the horror and devastation that was ahead, and frankly, it made him angry. It was true that Judah hadn't exactly been obeying everything God told them to do. In fact, he had come to the Lord to ask why He seemed to be allowing wickedness, strife and oppression to run rampant in Judah. Why didn't He step in and save the righteous?

But the Lord's response was not what he was hoping for. Instead of receiving reassurance about God's mercy or His plan to send revival that would turn the people back to Him, the Lord told Habakkuk that He was sending the Chaldeans to kill and plunder and enslave. Surely he couldn't have heard correctly! The Chaldeans were so much more wicked than the people of Judah! The Lord couldn't possibly use them for His purposes, could He? They should be the ones who would be destroyed, not God's chosen people of Judah.

So Habakkuk challenged the Lord's plan. "Why are You silent when the wicked swallow up those more righteous than they?" he asked (Hab. 1:13). "I don't think this is a good idea, God, and I want to know why you think it is." Habakkuk needed an answer. He needed to understand God's strategy if he was going to proclaim it to the people. He needed to hear from God. And he knew what he could do to prepare himself to hear God's voice:

"I will stand on my guard post and station myself on the rampart; and I will keep watch to see what He will speak to me, and how I may reply when I am reproved. Then the LORD answered me and said, 'Record the vision and inscribe it on tablets, that the one who reads it may run.'" (HAB. 2:1,2)

The Lord answered him. He assured Habakkuk that when He was done using the Chaldeans as an instrument of chastening for Judah, the Chaldeans themselves would be punished for their arrogance and sin (Hab.2:6-8). Though their choices for war and violence made them available for God's use, still, their actions would be judged.

Because he could see and hear from God, Habakkuk's faith was quickened. Trust was restored. Praise and worship rose from his heart: "[Your] radiance is like the sunlight...You went forth for the salvation of Your people...Though the fig tree should not blossom and there be no fruit on the vines, though the yield of the olive should fail and the fields produce no food, though the flock should be cut off from the fold and there be no cattle in the stalls, yet I will exult in the Lord, I will rejoice in the God of my salvation. The Lord God is my strength...." (Hab. 3)

Hearing from God changes everything, because it changes us.

HOW DO I HEAR GOD'S VOICE?

"My sheep hear My voice, and I know them, and they follow Me" (JOHN 10:27).

Did you know that you are now one of His sheep? That means that you have His promise that you can hear His voice! It is not an exclusive blessing reserved only for the most holy or the clergy or the mature or any other special people. The promise is that all of His sheep hear His voice and He knows them and they follow Him. This ability to hear and recognize God's voice is key to your new life. *"This is eternal life, that they might know You, the only true God, and Jesus Christ whom You have sent"* (John 17:3). How can you get to know God as your personal Lord, Savior, Father, Brother and Friend if you cannot hear Him speaking back to you when you talk to Him? All of Christian growth is through the working of the Spirit Who lives within you. The more acquainted you are with the Spirit—what He sounds like and feels like within you— the more responsive you will become to His guidance.

We have looked at so many incredible promises that God has given to us in our salvation, and they are all absolutely true. But many of them are in your life right now only in seed form. The potential for them to grow and bear fruit is there, but only if they are carefully tended. God is not a cosmic Santa Claus who magically drops gifts into your life. He is not a genie who grants your wishes. He is a Father Who wants to have a relationship with you so He can teach, guide, counsel, and comfort you. As you live in relationship with Him by daily having two-way conversations with Him, He will give you creative ideas for dealing with any problem or issue that comes your way. He will guide you in making decisions that bring blessing, peace and joy into your life.

He will protect you from potential harm. He will show you His perspective which is so much higher than yours.

The Christian life is about walking and living by the Spirit, working out our salvation because He is within us giving us the desire and the ability to please and obey Him. Hearing and recognizing His voice within you is vital to walking into all that has been provided for you through the cross and the New Covenant.

The problem is that we have become insensitive to the voice of the Spirit. The Bible indicates that He speaks in "a still, small voice" which means that it can easily be drowned out by the noise and activity of our daily lives. If we want to hear Him, we need to take the time to listen. And Habakkuk has given us a pattern that will help us out if we will follow it. Let's take a look at what he did.

"I WILL STAND ON MY GUARD POST"

Habakkuk recognized that he needed to come apart from the busy-ness of everyday life if he wanted to hear from God. Like us, he needed to quiet his own heart and mind so that he could tune in to the Holy Spirit. Psalm 46:10 encourages us to "Be still, slow down, cease striving, and know that I am God." In Revelation 1:10, John declares, "I was in the Spirit on the Lord's day, and I heard behind me a loud voice...." So the first key to hearing God's voice is to go to a quiet place free from the noise and distractions clamoring for your attention, and still your own thoughts and emotions.

Loving God through a quiet worship song is one very effective way to become still. In 2 Kings 3, Elisha needed a word from the Lord so he said, "Bring me a minstrel," and as the minstrel played, the Lord spoke. It is important to choose your song carefully; boisterous songs of praise will not bring you to stillness, but rather gentle songs that express your love and worship. And it isn't enough just to sing the song into the cosmos. Come into the Lord's presence by using your godly imagination to see the truth that He is right there with you, and sing your songs to Him, personally.

Praying in tongues can also be very helpful in bringing you to a quiet sense of God's presence.

"I WILL Keep Watch to see"

To receive the pure word of God, it is very important that your heart be properly focused as you become still, because your focus is the source of the intuitive flow. If you fix your eyes upon Jesus (Heb. 12:2), the intuitive flow comes from Jesus. But if you fix your gaze upon some desire of your heart, the intuitive flow comes out of that desire. To have a pure flow you must become still and carefully fix your spiritual eyes upon Jesus. Quietly worshiping the King and receiving out of the stillness that follows is a good way to keep your focus pure.

So the second key to hearing God's voice is to fix the eyes of your heart upon Jesus as you pray, seeing in the Spirit the dreams and visions of Almighty God. Habakkuk was actually looking for vision as he prayed. He opened the eyes of his heart, and looked into the spirit realm to see what God wanted to show him.

God has always spoken through dreams and visions, and He specifically said that they would come to those upon whom the Holy Spirit is poured out (Acts 2:1-4, 17). That means you!

He has given eyes in your heart to see in the spirit the vision and movement of Almighty God (Eph. 1:18). There is an active spirit world all around us, full of angels, demons, the Holy Spirit, the omnipresent Father, and His omnipresent Son, Jesus. The only reasons for us not to see this reality are unbelief or lack of knowledge.

In his sermon in Acts 2:25, Peter refers to King David's statement: "I saw the Lord always in my presence; for He is at my right hand, so that I will not be shaken." The original psalm makes it clear that this was a decision of David's, not a constant supernatural visitation: "I have set (literally, I have placed) the Lord continually before me; because He is at my right hand, I will not be shaken" (Ps.16:8). Because David knew that the Lord was always with him, he determined in his spirit to see that truth with the eyes of his heart as he went through life, knowing that this would keep his faith strong.

In order to see, we must look. Daniel saw a vision in his mind and said, "I was looking...I kept looking...I kept looking" (Dan. 7:2, 9, 13). As you pray, look for Jesus, and watch as He speaks to you, doing and saying the things that are on His heart. Most Christians will find that if they will only look, they will see. Jesus is Emmanuel, God with us (Matt. 1:23). It is as simple as that. You can see Christ present with you because Christ is present with you. In fact, the vision may come so easily that you will be tempted to reject it, thinking that it is just you. But if you persist in recording these visions, your doubt will soon be overcome by faith as you recognize that the content of them could only be birthed in Almighty God.

Jesus demonstrated the ability of living out of constant contact with God, declaring that He did nothing on His own initiative, but only what He saw the Father doing, and heard the Father saying (Jn. 5:19, 20, 30). What an incredible way to live!

Is it possible for us to live out of divine initiative as Jesus did? Yes! We must simply fix our eyes upon Jesus. The veil has been torn, giving access into the immediate presence of God, and He calls us to draw near (Lk. 23:45; Heb. 10:19-22). "I pray that the eyes of your heart will be enlightened..." (Eph. 1:18).

"WHAT HE WILL SPEAK TO ME"

Like Habakkuk, you can learn to recognize the sound of God speaking to you (Hab. 2:2). Elijah described it as a still, small voice (1 Kings 19:12). I had previously listened for an inner audible voice, and God does speak that way at times. However, I have found that usually God's voice comes as spontaneous thoughts, visions, feelings, or impressions.

Experience indicates that we perceive spirit-level communication as spontaneous thoughts, impressions and visions, and Scripture confirms this in many ways. For example, one definition of *paga*, a Hebrew word for intercession, is "a chance encounter or an accidental intersecting." When God lays people on our hearts, He does it through *paga*, a chance-encounter thought "accidentally" intersecting our minds.

So the third key to hearing God's voice is recognizing that God's voice in your heart often sounds like a flow of spontaneous thoughts. Therefore, when you want to hear from God, tune to chance-encounter or spontaneous thoughts. Your thoughts from your mind are analytical, cognitive, connected, built by you. The Spirit's voice is generally sensed as flowing thoughts which light upon your mind. Similarly, the Spirit's visions are generally sensed as flowing pictures which touch your heart and the Spirit's emotions are sensed as flowing emotions which come from deep within.

But how do you capture those spontaneous flowing thoughts? How can you be sure that they are really from God and not just your own mind?

"RECORD THE VISION"

Finally, God told Habakkuk to record the vision (Hab. 2:2). This was not an isolated command. The Scriptures record many examples of individual's prayers and God's replies, such as the Psalms, many of the prophets, and Revelation. You will find that obeying this final principle amplifies your confidence in your ability to hear God's voice so that you can make living out of His initiatives a way of life. The fourth key, two-way journaling or writing out your prayers and God's answers, brings great freedom in hearing God's voice.

Two-way journaling is a fabulous catalyst for clearly discerning God's inner, spontaneous flow, because as you journal you are able to write in faith for long periods of time, simply believing it is God. What you believe you have received from God must be tested. However, testing involves doubt and doubt blocks divine communication, so you don't want to test while you are trying to receive. (See James 1:5-8.) With journaling, you can receive in faith, knowing that when the flow has ended you can test and examine it carefully.

IS IT *really* GOD?

Here are five ways you can be sure what you're hearing is from Him:

- **Test the Origin (1 Jn. 4:1)**

  Thoughts from our own minds are progressive, with one thought leading to the next, however tangentially. Thoughts from the spirit world are spontaneous. The Hebrew word for true prophecy is *naba*, which literally means to bubble up, whereas false prophecy is *ziyd*, meaning to boil up. True words from the Lord will bubble up from our innermost being; we don't need to cook them up ourselves.

- **Compare It to Biblical Principles**

  God will never say something to you personally which is contrary to His universal revelation as expressed in the Scriptures. If the Bible clearly states that something is a sin, no amount of journaling can make it right. Much of what you journal about will not be specifically addressed in the Bible, however, so an understanding of biblical principles is also needed.

- **Compare It to the Names and Character of God as Revealed in the Bible**

  Anything God says to you will be in harmony with His essential nature. Journaling will help you get to know God personally, but knowing what the Bible says about Him will help you discern what words are from Him. Make sure the tenor of your journaling lines up with the character of God as described in the names of the Father, Son and Holy Spirit.

- **Test the Fruit (Matt. 7:15-20)**

    What effect does what you are hearing have on your soul and your spirit? Words from the Lord will quicken your faith and increase your love, peace and joy. They will stimulate a sense of humility within you as you become more aware of Who God is and who you are. On the other hand, any words you receive which cause you to fear or doubt, which bring you into confusion or anxiety, or which stroke your ego (especially if you hear something that is "just for you alone—no one else is worthy") must be immediately rebuked and rejected as lies of the enemy.

- **Share It with Your Spiritual Counselors (Prov. 11:14)**

    We are members of a Body! A cord of three strands is not easily broken and God's intention has always been for us to grow together. Nothing will increase your faith in your ability to hear from God like having it confirmed by two or three other people. Share it with your spouse, your parents, your friends, your elder, your group leader, even your grown children can be your sounding board. They don't need to be perfect or super-spiritual; they just need to love you, be committed to being available to you, have a solid biblical orientation, and most importantly, they must also willingly and easily receive counsel. Avoid the authoritarian who insists that because of their standing in the church or with God, they no longer need to listen to others. Find two or three people and let them confirm that you are hearing from God.

FOUR SIMPLE KEYS

Hearing God's voice is as simple as quieting yourself down, fixing your eyes on Jesus, tuning to spontaneity and writing (Hab. 2:1,2).

These four simple keys from Habakkuk have been used by people of all ages, from four to a hundred and four, from every continent, culture and denomination, to break through into intimate two-way conversations with their loving Father and dearest Friend. Omitting any one of the keys will prevent you from receiving all He wants to say to you. The order of the keys is not important, just that you *use them all.* Embracing all four, by faith, can change your life. Simply quiet yourself down, tune to spontaneity, look for vision, and journal. He is waiting to meet you there.

You will be amazed when you journal! Doubt may hinder you at first, but throw it off, reminding yourself that it is a biblical concept, and that God is present, speaking to His children. Relax. When we cease our labors and enter His rest, God is free to flow (Heb. 4:10).

Why not try it for yourself, right now? Sit back comfortably, take out your pen and paper, smile and picture yourself as a child (Mk. 10:14, 15). Turn your attention toward the Lord in praise and worship, seeking His face. Many people have found the music and visionary prayer called "A Stroll Along the Sea of Galilee" helpful in getting them started. You can listen to it and download it free at www.CWGMinistries.org/Galilee.

After you write your question to Him, become still, fixing your gaze on Jesus. You will suddenly have a very good thought. Don't doubt it; simply write it down. Later, as you read your journaling, you, too, will be blessed to discover that you are indeed dialoguing with God. If you wonder if it is really the Lord speaking to you, share it with your spouse or a friend. Their input will encourage your faith and strengthen your commitment to spend time getting to know the Lover of your soul more intimately than you ever dreamed possible.

ADDITIONAL RESOURCES

- *Dialogue with God*—Mark and Patti Virkler
- *Intimacy with the Holy Spirit*—Mark and Patti Virkler
- *Hosting the Presence*—Bill Johnson

PERSONAL APPLICATION

1. Prayerfully and with thanksgiving, read the following amazing promises given to everyone who will listen to and obey the voice of God:

> *And it shall come to pass, if you shall hearken diligently unto the voice of the LORD your God, to observe and to do all his commandments which I command you this day, that the LORD your God will set you on high above all nations of the earth:*
>
> **2 And all these blessings shall come on you, and overtake you, if you shall hearken unto the voice of the LORD your God.**
>
> *3 Blessed shall you be in the city, and blessed shall you be in the field.*
>
> *4 Blessed shall be the fruit of your body, and the fruit of your ground, and the fruit of your herds, the increase of your cattle, and the flocks of your sheep.*
>
> *5 Blessed shall be your basket and your kneading-trough.*
>
> *6 Blessed shall you be when you come in, and blessed shall you be when you go out.*

7 The LORD shall cause your enemies that rise up against you to be defeated before your face: they shall come out against you one way, and flee before you seven ways.

8 The LORD shall command the blessing upon you in your storehouses, and in all that you set your hand unto; and he shall bless you in the land which the LORD your God gives you.

9 The LORD shall establish you a holy people unto himself, as he has sworn unto you, if you shall keep the commandments of the LORD your God, and walk in his ways.

10 And all people of the earth shall see that you are called by the name of the LORD; and they shall be afraid of you.

11 And the LORD shall make you bountiful in goods, in the fruit of your body, and in the fruit of your cattle, and in the fruit of your ground, in the land which the LORD swore unto your fathers to give you.

12 The LORD shall open unto you his good treasure, the heaven to give the rain unto your land in its season, and to bless all the work of your hand: and you shall lend unto many nations, and you shall not borrow.

13 And the LORD shall make you the head, and not the tail; and you shall be above only, and you shall not be beneath; if that you hearken unto the commandments of the LORD your God, which I command you this day, to observe and to do them:

14 And you shall not go aside from any of the words which I command you this day, to the right hand, or to the left, to go after other gods to serve them.
(DEUTERONOMY 28:1-14 KJV)

Which promises are especially meaningful to you at this point in your life?

_____

_____

_____

_____

_____

2. *'AND IT SHALL BE IN THE LAST DAYS,' God says, '*
   THAT I WILL POUR FORTH OF MY SPIRIT
   ON ALL MANKIND;
   AND YOUR SONS AND YOUR DAUGHTERS
   SHALL PROPHESY,
   AND YOUR YOUNG MEN SHALL SEE VISIONS,
   AND YOUR OLD MEN SHALL DREAM DREAMS; (ACTS 2:17)

   This is part of Peter's sermon to the crowds that gathered after the disciples were baptized in the Holy Spirit and were heard speaking in tongues. Peter said that what they were hearing and seeing was what the prophet Joel was talking about in this passage.

   What is promised to accompany the coming of the gift of the Spirit?

   _____

   _____

   _____

3. King David said,

   'I SAW THE LORD ALWAYS IN MY PRESENCE; FOR
   HE IS AT MY RIGHT HAND, SO THAT I WILL NOT BE
   SHAKEN.'   (PSALM 16:8, ACTS 2:25)

An angel appeared to Joseph, who was engaged to Mary, the mother of Jesus and told him:

*"BEHOLD, THE VIRGIN SHALL BE WITH CHILD AND SHALL BEAR A SON, AND THEY SHALL CALL HIS NAME IMMANUEL," which translated means, **"GOD WITH US**."* (MATTHEW 1:23)

And the writer of the book of Hebrews reminds us:

*He Himself has said, **"I WILL NEVER DESERT YOU, NOR WILL I EVER FORSAKE YOU**," so that we confidently say, "THE LORD IS MY HELPER, I WILL NOT BE AFRAID. WHAT WILL MAN DO TO ME?"* (HEBREWS 13:5, 6)

There is absolutely no doubt that God is always with you. You never have to feel alone again. How would seeing the Lord always with you keep you from being shaken by the circumstances of life? What can you do to develop the lifestyle of seeing the Lord always with you?

---

4. Can you think of a time when you had a spontaneous, chance-encounter thought that you now realize was the Lord speaking to you?

---

5. Read James 1:5-8. What is required of one asks God for anything? How is the person described who does not meet that requirement?

_____

_____

_____

_____

6. *Where there is no guidance the people fall,*
   But in abundance of counselors there is victory.

   (PROVERBS 11:14)

   Remember what we learned in earlier chapters about being part of a family and members of the Body of Christ? God does not intend for us to live our Christian lives alone and unconnected from our brothers and sisters. Who has he placed in your life that you can depend on as counselors that you can share your two-way journaling with and to help you achieve victory in every area of your life?

   _____

   _____

   _____

7. State the four keys to hearing God's voice given in the chapter.

   _____

   _____

   _____

8. Use the free "A Stroll Along the Sea of Galilee" prayer (www. CWGMinistries.org/Galilee) to guide you into an experience of two-way conversation with your Lord. Be sure to use all four keys.

9. Choose a verse from this chapter that especially spoke to you to meditate on and hide in your heart.

GROUP ACTIVITIES

1. Share your answers to Applications 1–7.

2. Share your memory verses and why you chose them. What has the Lord especially ministered to you through them?

3. Enjoy a time of group journaling using the "Sea of Galilee" guided exercise. After 5—10 minutes for personal journaling, break into groups of two or three and share with each other your conversation with the Lord. (If what was spoken about was too personal to share, you can talk about something specific the Lord has done in your life through this course, especially through this lesson.)

   After about five minutes of small group sharing, draw the whole group back together and invite any who would like to read their two-way journaling to do so, so that everyone may be blessed by the words of the Lord.

4. Rejoice together in the amazing truth that the God of all creation wants to have a conversation with each one of us!

9

Walk in Love

God is love.... (1 JN. 4:16)

What an amazing statement: God is love! The essence of the Creator and Ruler of the Universe is Love. Over and over, throughout the Old and New Testaments, the love, compassion, mercy, care, kindness and tenderness of God toward us is proclaimed:

The steadfast love of the LORD never ceases; his mercies never come to an end; they are new every morning; great is your faithfulness. (LAM. 3:22)

The LORD is compassionate and gracious, Slow to anger and abounding in lovingkindness. (PS. 103:8)

"I have loved you with an everlasting love; Therefore, I have drawn you with lovingkindness." (JER. 31:3)

The LORD your God in the midst of you is mighty; he will save, he will rejoice over you with joy; he will quiet you with his love, he will rejoice over you with singing. (ZEPH. 3:17)

The eyes of the LORD move to and fro throughout the earth that He may strongly support those whose heart is completely His.

(2 CHRON. 16:9)

For I am convinced that neither death, nor life, nor angels, nor principalities, nor things present, nor things to come, nor powers, nor height, nor depth, nor any other created thing, will be able to separate us from the love of God, which is in Christ Jesus our Lord. (ROM. 8:38,39)

[I pray] that you, being rooted and grounded in love, may be able to comprehend with all the saints what is the breadth and length and height and depth, and to know the love of Christ which surpasses knowledge, that you may be filled up to all the fullness of God. (EPH. 3:17-19)

Are not two sparrows sold for a cent? And yet not one of them will fall to the ground apart from your Father. But the very hairs of your head are all numbered. So do not fear; you are more valuable than many sparrows. (MATT. 10:29-31)

Greater love has no one than this, that one lay down his life for his friends. (JN. 15:13)

What a wonderful Father you have! And as a child of God, you now have the DNA of love! Because you have joined yourself to the Lord, you are one spirit with Him (2 Cor. 6:17), and that Spirit is Love. You share the divine nature of love (2 Pet. 1:4).

God is love, and the one who abides in love abides in God, and God abides in him. (1 JN. 4:16)

Therefore, be imitators of God, as beloved children; and walk in love... (EPH. 5:1,2)

Jesus said, "A new commandment I give to you, that you love one another, even as I have loved you, that you also love one another. By this all men will know that you are My disciples, if you have love for one another." (JN.13:35, 36)

I...implore you to walk in a manner worthy of the calling with which you have been called, with all humility and gentleness, with patience, showing tolerance for one another in love, being diligent to preserve the unity of the Spirit in the bond of peace. (EPH. 4:1-3)

The love of God has been poured out within our hearts through the Holy Spirit who was given to us. (ROMANS 5:5)

Just as love is the defining characteristic of God, so it is now your defining characteristic. This is the essence of Christianity. The most powerful way that people will know that you are a child of God and a follower of Jesus is by your love for them. There are so many people who don't know about God's love. They feel like there is no one who loves them, that they are unlovable. But God has poured out His love into our hearts through the Holy Spirit and now we can be living expressions of His love for others.

What is love?

There are many beautiful Bible passages that describe how love is expressed, the most famous being 1 Corinthians 13:4-8:

Love is patient, love is kind and is not jealous; love does not brag and is not arrogant, does not act unbecomingly; it does not seek its own, is not provoked, does not take into account a wrong suffered, does not rejoice in unrighteousness, but rejoices with the truth; bears all things, believes all things, hopes all things, endures all things. Love never fails...."

Ephesians 4 calls us to be humble, gentle, patient, to show tolerance for one another and to do our best to preserve the unity of the Spirit in the bond of peace. We tell each other the truth and speak only words that build each other up. We put away all bitterness, anger, harsh words, slander and malice. We are kind to one another and tender-hearted, forgiving each other just as God has forgiven us.

Similar words are found in Colossians 3, where we are encouraged to walk in compassion, kindness, humility, gentleness and patience. We put aside all anger, wrath, malice, slander and abusive speech. We do not lie to one another and we forgive everyone of everything we might have against them.

Because of God's love, we accept one another just as Christ has accepted us (Rom. 15:7). We are gentle with the failings of others, and we carry each other's burdens (Gal. 6:1,2). We do nothing out of selfish ambition or empty pride, but in humility consider others as more important than ourselves. We don't look out for our own personal interests but also the interests of others (Phil. 2:3,4). We give preference to one another in honor; we bless those who persecute us; we overcome evil with good (Rom. 12:10,14,21). We are hospitable to one another. We use our gifts to serve each other (1 Pet. 4:9,10).

That is a description of the new you! Because the Holy Spirit has been joined to your spirit and you share the divine nature of God Himself, you are now love on the inside as well! God never expects us to do anything that He does not give us the ability to do by His Spirit. It is so important that you embrace this truth about yourself and that you begin to see yourself as filled with love.

HOW DO YOU WALK IN LOVE?

Beloved, let us love one another, for love is from God; and **everyone who loves is born of God and knows God. The one who does not love does not know God,** *for God is love.*　　(1 JN. 4:7)

Did you notice that there are two characteristics of the one who loves? He is both **born of God** and he **knows God**. The one who does not love does not know God. You have been born of God, so you have taken the first step. But now it is vitally important that you get to know God. When you deeply experience God's love for you, that love will begin to overflow on all those you touch. When you learn how He expresses His love for you—how He treats you— you will begin to express the same love to others. We love, because He first loves us (1 Jn. 4:19).

So we do not try to work up love for the unlovely. We don't just pretend to love by going through the motions of kindness and patience. Instead, we invest time getting to know our God. Missionary Heidi Baker has been called to share the love of God to "the least of these"—the rejected, destitute, and broken in some of the most difficult nations of the world. She believes that Love has to look like something—whether feeding the hungry or taking home an orphan or healing a sick person or raising the dead. Love is an action. And she has learned that the only way she has that kind of love to share is by spending many hours a day with the Lord. She fills up her love tank in God's presence so she has love to give away. Heidi knows that the only lasting fruit of ministry is born from intimacy with God.

GETTING TO KNOW HIM

There are many avenues you can use to get to know God, but every one requires you to spend time with Him. Of course, the first place you are going to start is by meditating on the Scriptures and what they reveal about Him. They will give you snapshots of how He has expressed His love to people throughout history and the Holy Spirit will bring verses to life that will especially speak to you.

But don't stop there, for Jesus Himself said that searching the Scriptures was not enough because they only testify about Him. We must be willing to actually go to Him and spend time with Him personally (Jn. 5:39, 40). The Greek word for "know" used in 1 John 4 doesn't mean simple intellectual knowledge or understanding but rather refers to intimate, experiential knowledge. It is not enough to know facts about God; we must become intimately acquainted with Him by having our own encounters with Him.

THROUGH TWO-WAY JOURNALING

Two-way journaling is an extremely powerful way for you to get to know the Lord. He will reveal Himself to you in ways that are personally designed to be most meaningful to you. He will affirm you and love you so much that at times you might not believe it is really God speaking because He is so nice to you!

Your journaling times are special to Him because what He wants most is to have a relationship with you, and journaling provides an effective avenue for that to happen. All too often we want Him to give us direction or insight or guidance but what He wants most to do is love on you. Your loving Him and giving Him a chance to love you is the central thing to Him—more essential than what you do or how you act or anything else that we try to make important. Take the time to let Him love you every day so you are so filled up with His love that it spills over onto everyone you meet.

THROUGH DREAMS

Dreams are another central way that we can get to know God. Dreams are God's contingency plan, giving Him a way to connect with every single person, no matter what their beliefs about Him may be. Throughout the Bible, God used dreams to speak to people to give direction, encouragement, wisdom and revelation.

He talks with *you* through your dreams, too, but you might need to learn the symbolic language that He uses to communicate His messages. Dreams are a strategic avenue by which God can touch your heart and help you to really feel His love for you.

In her powerful book, *Hearing God Through Your Dreams*, my daughter Charity Kayembe shares a beautiful dream by one of her students in which she was at a ball. A famous actor who always played heroic roles was there and this actor chose the dreamer as his partner for every dance. She felt incredibly special that he would seek her out from all the other people there and want to share every dance with her. She awoke, still carrying that cherished feeling, and the Lord told her that it was He Who was choosing her, caring for her and dancing with her.

Her dream allowed her to *feel* how special she is to God in a way that mere theological understanding never could. Your dreams are a wonderful gift from the Lord through which you can deepen your experiential knowledge of Him.

When you lie down in bed tonight, ask the Lord to give you a dream that will show you how He sees you. As soon as you awaken, record your dream or you will quickly forget it. Even if it doesn't make sense to you, ask the Lord through two-way journaling to interpret it for you so you can receive His message to you. Explore the fascinating world of hearing God through your dreams by seeking instruction and guidance from those ahead of you in the Lord. (Recommended resources to help you can be found at the end of the chapter.)

THROUGH MEDITATION

When we talked about biblical meditation, we saw that it included pondering, reflecting, rolling over and over in your mind, and using your imagination. When the Lord reveals something to you about Himself, and especially about His love for you, it is important that you meditate on it if you want that truth to become flesh in you.

If you simply see the truth, get happy about it for a moment, thank God for showing it to you, then move on to the next thing, you will forget it and it will not have a lasting impact on you. By meditating, pondering, reflecting and picturing the truth, you are shaped and changed by it. For example, the lady who dreamed of dancing could call up that dream in her mind and feel again the joy of being chosen and cherished. Meditating on the message of God to her through the dream increased its power to transform her the way God intended.

So when the Lord gives you a dream or speaks through your journal or the Scriptures or a sermon, stop and really look at that truth. Engage all your senses, looking to see what the Spirit will reveal, listening to hear what He will say. If you want to get to know God's love for you, for example, take some time to meditate on the verses at the beginning of this chapter, or these precious words:

The eternal God is your refuge, and underneath are the everlasting arms. (DEUT. 33:27 NIV)

Or again:

"Can a woman forget her nursing child and have no compassion on the son of her womb? Even these may forget, but I will not forget you. Behold, I have inscribed you on the palms of My hands."   (IS. 49:15,16)

Open the eyes of your heart to see what that love looks like. How is God showing His love to you? What does it mean that God is your refuge? What does it feel like to be held in His everlasting arms? What do God's hands look like with your picture on them? How does it feel to be loved that much? Stay in that place of meditation; experience the truth of God's Word. Throughout the next week, recall and reflect on what the Lord shows you. Roll it over and over in your mind like a cow chewing her cud, until it becomes a part of you.

THROUGH WORSHIP

Spending time in worship, especially throne room worship, is another way to experience the love of God. Using the eyes of your heart as you come into His presence, you can see Him and interact with Him in amazing ways. One worshiper shared, "During a period of time in which I had been fervently seeking to know the Father's heart, I saw the saints of Heaven dancing joyfully in praise to the Father. Then, to my utter amazement and delight, I saw the Father join them in the dancing, as a loving earthly father joins his little children in dancing at a wedding, for example. My heart filled with joy as I caught a glimpse into our Heavenly Father's beautiful heart." The Lord will give you precious moments with Him, as well, letting you know Him better each day.

Worshipping often involves music, so the next time you are singing a song of worship, pay attention to the words. Usually they will be descriptive about God or some aspect of His character or something that He has done for us. Open the eyes of your heart to imagine the truth that is being sung. See the images you are singing about. If there is no special picture that is suggested, see yourself before the throne of God, joining with the saints and angels, bowing in His presence. Don't let your worship be words only but enter in with your whole heart. As you offer the eyes of your heart to the Spirit, He will give you amazing and delightful visions of the spirit world.

These ways of spending time with Jesus will blend and merge as the Spirit leads you. You may awaken from a dream and ask the Lord through journaling what it means. As He reveals His love to you, you may find yourself overwhelmed with worship, which draws you deeper into His presence. As you linger there, soaking in His love, He will continue to speak and reveal things to you. You meditate on what He says, seeing, hearing, feeling, experiencing that truth.

The key is giving Him time. You can't rush into His presence, blurt out your prayer requests and hurry away to your "important" life and expect to walk in love. You must be filled up with His love so much that it overflows on everyone you touch.

WALK IN LOVE

What does it mean to walk in love? We have already looked at many of the characteristics that will be expressions of our love as we extend God's love to others. Heidi Baker encourages us to "stop for the one"—to just love the person who is right there in front of you.

Ask God to let you see each person you meet through His eyes, and love will rise up within you. Ask Him what He wants to say to them or do for them, then do it. It may be a word of encouragement or a prayer. It may be a hug or a helping hand. It doesn't matter if it seems to be a big thing or a little thing to us; if it flows from a heart of compassion and meets their need, it is a touch from God Who is Love.

ADDITIONAL RESOURCES

- *From the Father's Heart*—Charles Slagle
- *Hearing God Through Your Dreams*—Mark Virkler and Charity Kayembe
- *Hosting the Presence*—Bill Johnson
- *Grace and Forgiveness*—John and Carol Arnott

PERSONAL APPLICATION

1. Choose at least one of the verses about God's great love for you and meditate on it according to the pattern given in Chapter 5.

2. Read Ephesians 4 and Colossians 3. What expressions of love are most important to you? What ones do you need the Holy Spirit to help you express?

-----

3. Spend at least ten minutes in two-way journaling every day this week. Use all four keys. Record your conversations. Get to know your God.

4. Put a notebook and pen beside your bed. When you lie down, ask the Lord to give you a dream. As soon as you awaken, record your dream or you will quickly forget it. Even if it doesn't make sense to you, ask the Lord through two-way journaling to interpret it for you so you can receive His message to you. (You can wait until morning to journal about the interpretation, but if you do not record the dream as soon as you awaken from it—even if it is the middle of the night— by morning the message will be lost.)

5. If you haven't done so already, take some time to meditate on these verses:

    > *The eternal God is your refuge, and underneath are the everlasting arms.* (DEUT. 33:27 NIV)

    > *"Can a woman forget her nursing child and have no compassion on the son of her womb? Even these may forget, but I will not forget you. Behold, I have inscribed you on the palms of My hands."* (IS. 49:15,16)

    Open the eyes of your heart to see what that love looks like. How is God showing His love to you? What does it mean that God is your refuge? What does it feel like to be held in His everlasting arms? What do God's hands look like with your picture on them? How does it feel to be loved that much? Stay in that place of meditation; experience the truth of God's Word.

------

6. Spend some time worshipping the Lord with your whole heart. It can be in a church service or alone in your home. Immerse yourself in the words and images that you are singing. Ask the Holy Spirit to open the eyes of your heart to show you whatever He wants you to see as you are in His presence. Later, when you are back in the material world, record what you saw and heard and experienced so you can come back and meditate on it, allowing it to seep deep into your heart.

------

7. Deliberately offer God an opportunity to love through you. After spending time with Him, go someplace where there are people who need a touch of His love. (That would be anywhere there are people.) When you go, ask the Lord to let you see each person you meet through His eyes. Ask Him what He wants you to say to them or do for them, then do it. "Stop for the one," and love whoever is right in front of you. It doesn't need to be a long experiment, but you may find it so fulfilling to feel God's love flowing through you and out on another that you might not want to stop!

8. Choose at least one of the beautiful verses about God's love for you from this chapter to memorize.

GROUP ACTIVITIES

1. Share your answers to the questions and your experiences in loving God and people.

2. Share your memory verses and why you chose that verse. What did God minister to you through it?

3. Have a time of journaling together according to the pattern in the Group Activities of Chapter 9.

4. Your group may want to go together to a park or mall or concert and do Application #7 as a group. Come together afterward to share your experiences and rejoice in the love of God shed abroad in your hearts.

10

The Law of the Lord

Now that He is living within you, you are beginning to hear Him speaking to you in gentle, flowing thoughts that are not your own. Deep within you will hear a voice saying, "This is the way; walk in it" (Isa.30:21). He will begin to guide your steps into a life that not only pleases Him but that fills you with love, joy and peace that exceeds all understanding. And He will reveal more of His great love for you and His desire to spend time together with you.

You have already heard His voice, for He is the One who has brought you to the place of salvation. It is He who has drawn you to Himself (Jn. 6:44). Expect that He will continue to speak to you. Take time to listen for His voice. Keep the Lord continuously before you by seeing Him always with you (Acts 2:25; Ps. 16:8). Set aside time each day just to have a conversation with Him. Knowing God—that's what you were created for and why you were redeemed.

One of the things God will speak about is removing sinful thoughts and behaviors from your life because they are destructive to you, your relationships, and the fulfillment of His destiny for you. This is considered the outworking of your initial salvation experience (Phil. 2:12). It is the laying down of your life, dying to self and coming progressively alive to the workings of the Holy Spirit within you.

His design is for the Spirit's power to flow through you to others. You can and will manifest the Holy Spirit who is living within you (1 Cor. 12:7-11). So let's talk about how to give God the opportunity to remove the sins within you which can hinder His flow and impede the fulfillment of His destiny for your life. The removing of these sins is one of the evidences that you are His and His Spirit indwells you (Rom. 8:9-14; 2 Cor. 3:18; Gal. 5:16-25; Eph. 4:22-32; 1 Jn. 1:5-10; 2 Pet. 1:2-11).

WHAT IS SIN?

The Greek word translated as "sin" in the New Testament literally means "to miss the mark (and so not share in the prize)." Imagine you are taking part in an archery contest. You watch as your competitors take their best shots. Many of them do fairly well but there is one who consistently hits right in the center of the bullseye. You can't do better than that, but you can at least share first place if you can do as well as he did and hit the center of the goal every time you shoot. But, even though you have practiced for hours and you do your very best, you miss the mark. You are slightly off center, and sometimes you don't even hit the target. You won't be sharing in the prize. That is the picture of what sin is.

But what was the goal? What was the "mark" that you missed? It is perfect obedience to the Lord, living a holy life fully devoted to doing His will. In its simplest form, sin is doing something God said not to do, or not doing something God said to do. It is disobedience to the voice, commands or laws of God.

Jesus is the only One Who has ever perfectly hit the goal of obeying God and doing His will. All the rest of us have sinned, or missed the mark, and fallen short of the glory of God (Rom. 3:23). That is why Jesus was able to be our sacrifice and take the consequences of our sin: because He had no sin of His own for which He had to pay.

WHY DID GOD GIVE US LAWS TO OBEY?

Unfortunately, many people seem to see God as a crotchety old man who likes to make lots of rules that are designed to ruin all our fun. They see His laws as unreasonable restrictions on our behavior with no real purpose except to see if we will obey them. They are the arbitrary decrees of a power-hungry dictator who is just waiting to punish us when we fail to keep them.

Even as believers, we often fail to understand why obeying God is so important. Yes, we obey Him because He is our Lord and we have submitted our lives to Him. Yes, we obey Him because we love Him and want to please Him. But why did God give us the rules and laws in the first place? Are they just tests of our love? Is He really just a tyrant Who demands that His subjects obey His commands if they want to avoid His displeasure and receive His blessings? Nothing could be further from the truth! Knowing all that you do about God's love for you, it must be clear that His laws are also given out of love and a desire for what is best for you.

According to Galatians 3:23-25, the laws of God serve one of two purposes: to keep us safe and pure until we come to faith in Christ, or to reveal Christ to us, drawing us into a relationship with Him. God's commands are always designed for our good. Many of the Old Testament ceremonial laws were designed to

YOUR *EXTRAORDINARY* LIFE

prepare God's people for the coming of Christ and to help them understand the importance of His death and resurrection. Those ceremonial laws were fulfilled in Christ and we are no longer under obligation to keep them (Matt. 5:17, Hebrews 10:1-18).

Other commands in the Old Testament were given for physical health, such as the laws for quarantining certain sicknesses. When the people obeyed God's laws, they enjoyed better health and avoided the diseases of surrounding nations. When they received that law, they didn't understand the science behind it as we do today, but when they obeyed, they were protected.

Most of the commands we find in the New Testament are for our spiritual and relational well-being. When we obey them, our lives are richer and healthier and more peaceful. But just because we don't know the specific purpose for one of God's laws doesn't mean that it is not for our good or that we don't need to obey it.

Punished For Breaking the Law?

Let's take a look at one of God's laws that we all appreciate. The law of gravity is a good law serving many important purposes. Complaining that the only reason God made the law is because He wants to keep us walking around on the ground would be ignorant and ridiculous. Saying that He punished you by making you fall when you tried to go against His law would be just as absurd. God doesn't need to punish you if you try to "break" the law of gravity by stepping off the roof of a tall building. You are not "punished" for your actions; you are "punished" by your actions.

In the same way, God didn't punish the Israelites by making more of their people sick if they didn't obey His laws of quarantine.

That was a natural consequence of their actions. That is why God gave the law—because He knew what would happen if they let sick people live among the healthy. It is not His punishment when relationships are broken because we lie. He knew that honesty was one of the foundations for healthy relationships so He said, "Do not lie." It is not His punishment if you lose your family because of drunkenness. He knew the effects of alcohol on the body and the destructive behaviors that result. He knew the consequences that would follow a life of drunkenness so He said, "Do not get drunk."

When God created man and woman, He designed it so that when they come together they become one flesh (Gen. 2:24, 1 Cor. 6:16). It is not merely a physical act; God has fashioned it as supernatural "superglue" that unites them. No matter what our culture has tried to make us believe, physical intimacy involves much more than just our bodies. Soul ties are created and spirits united.

Jesus said, "They are no longer two, but one flesh" (Mk. 10:8). And when this mystical union takes place outside of the covenant of marriage, there are consequences. That bond was created as a good thing—to strengthen the marriage covenant, to increase your pleasure in each other's company, and to provide stability for children, just for starters. The union cannot be ignored without pain and brokenness. That is not God's punishment; it is jumping out of an airplane without a parachute.

ENLIGHTENED SELF-INTEREST

Every one of God's commands is given from a heart of love with our good in mind. Obeying them will lead you into that abundant, uncommon, extraordinary, remarkable life that you have been promised. Being patient, gentle and kind to other people will lay a foundation for loving, healthy relationships. Processing your anger before the Lord every day so that no bitterness or unforgiveness can build up protects your body from the toxins that they carry which can destroy your health. Telling the truth in love and speaking only words that encourage each other will enhance every relationship. Abstaining from greed, drunkenness and immorality protects you from the consequences that must follow them. Giving ten percent of your income to the Lord and sharing liberally with the poor release financial prosperity. Refraining from gluttony and heeding the dietary principles God has given keep your body from many sicknesses and diseases.

Following God's instructions in every area of your life will make your life better! You will be happier, healthier and enjoy more peaceful, loving relationships. Even if you didn't love God and want to please Him with your obedience, your own enlightened self-interest should compel you to embrace His words!

THE LAW OF THE LORD IS GOOD!

So, living a holy lifestyle of putting off sin begins with an understanding of why you would want to do so. God's commands are good! As the Psalmist declared:

> *The law of the LORD is perfect, restoring the soul;*
> *The testimony of the LORD is sure, making wise the simple.*

> *The precepts of the LORD are right, rejoicing the heart;*
> *The commandment of the LORD is pure, enlightening the eyes.*

The fear of the LORD is clean, enduring forever;
  The judgments of the LORD are true; they are
  righteous altogether.

They are more desirable than gold, yes, than much fine gold;
  Sweeter also than honey and the drippings of the honeycomb.

Moreover, by them Your servant is warned;
  In keeping them there is great reward.   (PS. 19:7- 11)

Teach me, O LORD, the way of Your statutes,
  And I shall observe it to the end.

Give me understanding, that I may observe Your law
  And keep it with all my heart.

Make me walk in the path of Your commandments,
  For I delight in it.

So I will keep Your law continually,
  Forever and ever.

And I will walk at liberty,
  For I seek Your precepts.

The law of Your mouth is better to me
  Than thousands of gold and silver pieces.

I will never forget Your precepts,
  For by them You have revived me.

Those who love Your law have great peace,
  And nothing causes them to stumble.

                    (PS. 119:33-35, 44, 45, 93, 165)

ADDILIONAL RESOURCES

- *Go Natural*—Mark and Patti Virkler
- *Fulfill Your Financial Destiny*—Mark and Patti Virkler
- *4 Reasons I Love to Fast*—Charity Kayembe
  (youtu.be/2MSeO5HN0iA)

PErSONAL APPLICATION

1. Slowly and prayerfully read through these verses that were
   referred to in the chapter:

   > But we all, with unveiled face, beholding as in a mirror
   > the glory of the Lord, are being transformed into the same
   > image from glory to glory, [which comes from] the Lord,
   > the Spirit   (2 CORINTHIANS 3:18)

   > If by the Spirit you are putting to death the deeds of the
   > body, you will live.   (ROMANS 9:13)

   > But I say, walk by the Spirit, and you will not carry out
   > the desire of the flesh. For the flesh sets its desire against
   > the Spirit, and the Spirit against the flesh; for these are in
   > opposition to one another, so that you may not do the things
   > that you please. But if you are led by the Spirit, you are not
   > under the Law. Now the deeds of the flesh are evident, which
   > are: immorality, impurity, sensuality, idolatry, sorcery,
   > enmities, strife, jealousy, outbursts of anger, disputes,
   > dissensions, factions, envying, drunkenness, carousing, and
   > things like these, of which I forewarn you, just as I have
   > forewarned you, that those who practice such things will not
   > inherit the kingdom of God. But the fruit of the Spirit is
   > love, joy, peace, patience, kindness, goodness, faithfulness,

*gentleness, self-control; against such things there is no law.
Now those who belong to Christ Jesus have crucified the flesh
with its passions and desires.*

If we live by the Spirit, let us also walk by the Spirit.

(GALATIANS 5:16-25)

*In reference to your former manner of life, you lay aside
the old self, which is being corrupted in accordance with
the lusts of deceit, and that you be renewed in the spirit of
your mind, and put on the new self, which in the likeness
of God has been created in righteousness and holiness of
the truth.* (EPHESIANS 4:22-24)

What does the Lord want to say to you personally through
these Scriptures?

_____

_____

_____

_____

2. Spend some time meditating on and journaling about the
    Psalms given at the end of the chapter. Ask the Holy Spirit
    to speak to you about the Laws of God so you may have an
    unshakable conviction concerning their goodness.

    _____

    _____

    _____

3. If you are interested in learning God's laws concerning money
    and finances, here are some verses for you to meditate on that
    will get you started. Be sure to journal about how the Lord
    wants to apply what you learn to your own life.

Proverbs 10:22

Psalm 35:27

Isaiah 48:17

Proverbs 13:21, 22

Proverbs 13:11

Proverbs 22:16

Proverbs 22:26, 27

Proverbs 13:18

Malachi 3:8-12

Luke 6:38

Deuteronomy 8:18

Proverbs 22:4

3 John 1:2

Proverbs 28:13

Proverbs 6:9-11

Proverbs 23:20, 21

Proverbs 21:5

Ecclesiastes 5:10

Proverbs 3:9, 10

Proverbs 28:27

_____

_____

_____

_____

_____

4. If you are interested in learning God's laws concerning health and healing, here are some verses for you to meditate on that will get you started. Be sure to journal about how the Lord wants to apply what you learn to your own life.

Genesis 1:26-31

Leviticus 11:9-12

Exodus 15:26

Proverbs 17:22

3 John 1:2

Genesis 9:3, 4

Daniel 1:8

Isaiah 58:8

James 5:14, 15

_____

_____

_____

_____

_____

5. If you are interested in learning God's laws concerning relationships, here are some verses for you to meditate on that will get you started. Be sure to journal about how the Lord wants to apply what you learn to your own life.

Galatians 6:2   Philippians 2:3, 4
Colossians 3:8, 9, 12-14   James 1:19-21
James 4:11   James 2:15-17
1 Peter 3:8, 9   1 Peter 4:8, 9
1 John 3:17, 18

_____

_____

_____

_____

6. If you are interested in learning God's laws concerning family relationships, here are some verses for you to meditate on that will get you started. Be sure to journal about how the Lord wants to apply what you learn to your own life. (Remember that the principles for relationships in #5 apply to family relationships as well!)

Ephesians 5:22-33   Ephesians 4:25-27, 29, 31, 32
Ephesians 4:1-4   Colossians 3:18-21
1 Thessalonians 4:3-7   1 Peter 3:1-7

_____

_____

_____

_____

_____

GROUP ACTIVITIES

1. Share your answers to the questions. Discuss what each one has learned and what the Lord has said personally to the individuals. Encourage one another to love and good works.

2. Have a time of journaling together according to the pattern in the Group Activities of Chapter 9.

11

Overcoming

You have been given a new heart and a new spirit that desires to please God. Your old man has died with Christ and you are a new creation who delights to do God's will. The power of sin is broken in your life and you are now able to resist temptation to do wrong and choose to do what you know is right. You know God personally and have experienced His great love for you, so you understand that any command or law He gives is for your benefit. You know that your life is happier, healthier, more filled with peace and joy, more fulfilled when you live the way He wants you to.

Now that Jesus is your Lord and the Holy Spirit is living within you, you will have already noticed some changes in your life. Sinful habits may have simply dropped away without any effort on your part. Your tastes may have changed in regard to the things that entertain you or make you laugh. Physical appetites for things that defile your body may suddenly disappear. Your speech may be so suddenly purified and seasoned with grace that those around you can't help but notice. These are miracles of the new life you have been given! Whenever you notice such a cleansing in your life, be sure to take the time to say, "Thank You!" to the One who has done this for you.

But some changes are a process. Though we may wish it were different, the Lord does not make us instantly perfect and impervious to all temptations. Some temptations will remain and you will be tempted to give in to them and live the way you have always lived. These temptations are opportunities for you to reaffirm your decision to make Jesus the Ruler of your life. He does not force you to follow His good plan for you because He has created you with free will. He wants you to obey because that is what you want to do, what you choose to do.

He leaves these remaining temptations so that you will learn to drive them out by the power of His Spirit as part of your training. And every temptation to sin can become an opportunity to strengthen your resolve and declare, "I am no longer in charge of my life. I made a mess of it all. Jesus is my Ruler now, and I will obey Him."

BY THE SPIRIT

When you are tempted, you have three choices:

1. You may just give in and sin.

2. You may try to resist the temptation in your own strength by setting your will to overcome.

3. You may turn to the Holy Spirit within you for the grace (the desire and strength) to resist.

You have already decided that number one is not really an option you are willing to consider. You are dead to sin, obeying God brings great reward, and you are not going to be moved from your new way of living. So when you are tempted by anything from your old life that you know is not pleasing to God or beneficial to your abundant life, you will choose to resist.

But how you resist will determine how successful you are. We all want to believe that we have the power to do whatever we decide to do, so we think if we just set our will, we will be able to live the Christian life. But that is not what Christianity is about at all!

First of all, let's face it—you have proven in your life up until now that you are not able to resist temptation on your own. How many New Year's Resolutions have you broken in the past? How many times have you promised yourself or someone you love that you will change, only to fall right back into the same destructive behaviors? And that was when you were just trying to live according to your own standards, which, you must admit, were quite a bit lower than God's. There is no way that you yourself, by the power of your own will, can attain to the life of holiness that God desires for you.

Thank God, that is not what He is asking you to do. You are not living on your own anymore. You have the Holy Spirit living within you who has all the power you need to overcome any temptation. He doesn't want you to try to clean yourself up to prove you are a Christian or to try to be good enough for Him to love and accept. All He wants you to do is cry, "Help me, Jesus!" and He will be there providing a way of escape (1 Cor. 10:13).

*"If **by the Spirit** you are putting to death the deeds of the body, you will live"* (ROMANS 8:13).

Living the Christian life has nothing to do with the strength of your will or the power of your own personality. It is not a self-improvement program in which you work hard at becoming righteous and loving and gentle and forgiving and all those other laws we talked about in the last chapter. Living the Christian life, resisting temptation, and walking in holiness are all about recognizing who you are and Who God is within you. God is not offering you a self-improvement program but a replacement program.

It was Satan, in the Garden of Eden, who said, "You can be like God." He is the one who is constantly telling you to establish in yourself godlike characteristics. Pray hard and work hard to become what you want to become or you think you should become. Try, try, try! God never once tells you in the Bible to try harder to be like Him. He knows it is impossible and He is waiting for you to accept that fact, as well.

Remember we said that Jesus was the only One who had always perfectly "hit the mark," the only One who has perfectly kept all of God's laws? Well, the Good News is that He is now living inside you through the power of the Holy Spirit! So you have the ability to resist temptation and live a life of holiness and power—if you will turn from dependence on yourself to dependence on Him. His strength is made perfect in your weakness (2 Cor. 12:9). When you can't do it yourself, He has the chance to do it for you.

WHILE WE LOOK

"But we all, with unveiled face, beholding as in a mirror the glory of the Lord, are being transformed into the same image from glory to glory, [which comes from] the Lord, the Spirit"
(2 CORINTHIANS 3:18).

If you look to yourself and your own willpower to resist temptation, you will often fail. Instead, look at the glory of the

Lord Who lives within you. See Him when you look at yourself, as if you were looking in a mirror that shows you the truth about who you really are now. You have been created anew, born of the Father, sharing the divine nature, joined to the Holy Spirit. Call out to Him to live through you and be whatever you need in the moment. Recognize your weakness and trust in His strength.

- **Look to see what Jesus is doing.** Picture Jesus present with you (Acts 2:25; Ps. 16:8). Use your godly imagination to see what is true. Then pray and ask the Holy Spirit to bring the scene alive (Eph. 1:17-18). Now tune to spontaneous flowing images, flowing thoughts, flowing emotions and flowing power/energy. These are Jesus' voice, vision, emotion and power coming to you through the Holy Spirit.

- **Say "Yes" to what Jesus is doing.** Seeing Jesus releases His presence, strength, glory and wisdom into the situation. You will not fall into the sin which you were tempted to commit. You see what Jesus is doing. You hear what He is saying. He obviously is not committing sin, and He is showing you how to resist as well. You watch Jesus in action and then do what you see Him doing.

- **Record what Jesus is speaking and doing.** In your devotional times you can expand this flow of His voice and His vision by simply writing it down as it is coming to you.

- **Confirm it.** Confirm that what you have written is actually from God by sharing it to a spiritual friend and comparing it to Scripture (1 Thess. 5:20-21; 2 Cor. 13:1). You will discover most of the time this flow is the voice of the Holy Spirit who flows within you as a River of Life.

Let's Get Practical

What does this look like in real life? Your grouchy co-worker lights into you over something insignificant, insulting and degrading you in front of your staff. Immediately your flesh wants to slap him back, maybe physically but at least verbally. However, you remember a command from the Bible that says,

> *But I tell you not to resist an evil person. But whoever slaps you on your right cheek, turn the other to him also*
> (MATT. 5:39).

Oh, great, you have to try to love him! So you try. And you try. And you try. But for all your trying, you still want to smack him. You find yourself harboring anger toward this individual, no matter how hard you "will" to love him and forgive him.

Then you remember Galatians 3:3.

> *Are you so foolish? Having begun in the Spirit, are you now being made perfect by the flesh?* (GAL. 3:3)

Of course! You know better than to behave like this! You were saved, not by your efforts, but by the work of the Holy Spirit. Do you really think you can now perfect yourself through your efforts rather than the Holy Spirit's? Of course not! "Lord, I am sorry for such foolishness. I repent."

Now you have it:

> *No temptation has overtaken you except such as is common to man; but God [is] faithful, who will not allow you to be tempted beyond what you are able, **but with the temptation will also make the way of escape**, that you may be able to bear [it]* (1 COR. 10:13).

"Lord, You have provided the way of escape, and I remember what that way is."

I have been crucified with Christ; it is no longer I who live, but Christ lives in me; and the [life] which I now live in the flesh I live by faith in the Son of God, who loved me and gave Himself for me (GAL. 2:20).

"You have replaced my old self, and now it is the life of Jesus that addresses this situation, not me at all."

Looking unto Jesus, the author and finisher of [our] faith... (HEB. 12:2).

"Lord Jesus, I come to You. I fix my eyes upon You. Please give me a vision of You handling this situation."

"My child, remember when My enemies unjustly accused Me, and beat Me and whipped Me and hung Me on a cross naked and bruised. Remember how I looked down on them from that cross and said to them, 'Father, forgive them, for they know not what they do.' So, too, My child, you have been unjustly accused and humiliated in public, but so, too, My love flows through your heart to forgive your adversaries. See My love flowing through your heart as you speak My words. See and you shall be whole. See, My child."

"Yes, my Lord, I see Your love flowing through me to those who have offended me and treated me unjustly, and I speak Your words again: 'Father, forgive them, for they don't know what they are doing.'

"Lord, I feel a change taking place within me. You are breaking the harshness and filling me with Your love. Thank You, my Lord. Thank You for Your wonderful power. I worship You."

123

Did you follow all the parts? They were:

1. You experience a hurt.

2. You see a command telling you how to respond.

3. You try to obey the command and realize you can't.

4. You remember not to try in the flesh but to look to the Spirit.

5. You remember that there is a way of escape through Jesus Christ.

6. You remember that Christ is in you and is living through you.

7. You fix your eyes on Jesus within you and ask Him to respond.

8. He responds with vision, *rhema* and power.

9. You say what He tells you to say and sense His power beginning to flow within your heart.

10. You begin to worship.

Of course, ideally you would jump right from number one to number seven and not waste time trying to "be a good Christian" on your own.

Drive Out the Darkness

Let me say it another way: Since Christ is the Light of the world, and sin is usually represented by darkness, we shall let light represent Christ and darkness represent the temptation. How do you combat darkness? By pushing it out of the room? Of course not. But that is how many of us try to combat sin in our lives. We kick at it and beat it and try to drive it out. How insane! If you saw me inside a darkened room kicking at the darkness and commanding it to go, you would lock me up.

Instead, we simply need to turn on the light! How? By coming to the God who has taken up residence within us and asking Him to reveal Himself to us in the midst of the situation. What are His words? What is His vision of the scene? Jesus said, "The words I have spoken to you are Spirit and are life" (John 6:63 NASB and Greek text). With His words and vision comes a flow of Spirit life that sets you free from the law of sin and death, and allows you to live supernaturally united to the Spirit of God and fused to Glory.

Love Your Enemies

Instead of saying, "Lord, I am trying to love that person. Please help me," you will be saying, "God, I can't love that person, but You can. You are Love and the Source of all love in the universe and You live within me. I ask you to flow out through me and love that person with Your supernatural love."

Fix your eyes on Jesus. Ask Him to show you how He sees the person you are struggling to love. Ask to see them through His eyes and His heart. Watch what He is saying to you and to them. As you do, you will begin to sense *agape* love welling up within you, energizing your inner man and transforming your feelings from within. You will begin to worship as God's love bubbles up and flows out through you effortlessly. Truly Christianity is supernatural after all!

We have given examples so far about loving and forgiving because they are issues that every one of us faces. But the principles are true for whatever temptation you face. Rather than trying to resist indulging in that habit the Lord has asked you to break, when the desire hits you, immediately cry out, "Jesus, help me. I cannot resist on my own. Thank you that your Spirit is within me giving me supernatural power to please you. Thank you that the old man that enjoyed these things is dead and buried and has no more power over me." Begin to worship your Savior for all He has done for you and the power of the temptation will diminish and disappear. The Light will grow brighter within you and the darkness will flee. *"Submit therefore to God. Resist the devil and he will flee from you. Draw near to God and He will draw near to you" (James 4:7, 8).*

PUT OFF, PUT ON

Simply remembering that the Lord is with you and in you, and calling out to Him to help you, often releases the strength you need to be victorious. But sometimes we have sinful habits that just seem to want to maintain their control over us. One of the ways the Spirit will show you how to overcome these sins is through putting off sin and putting on righteousness. Rather than simply trying to stop doing something that is wrong, He will give you a replacement for it that is godly so there is not a void in your life. Here are some biblical examples:

> *"Lay aside the old self, and put on the new self. Therefore, laying aside falsehood, speak truth each one of you with his neighbor. He who steals must steal no longer; but rather he must labor. Let no unwholesome word proceed from your mouth, but only such a word as is good for edification according to the need of the moment, so that it will give grace to those who hear. Do not grieve the Holy Spirit of God, by whom you were sealed for the day of redemption. Let all bitterness and wrath and anger and clamor and slander be put away from you, along with all malice.*

Be kind to one another, tender-hearted, forgiving each other, just as God in Christ also has forgiven you." (EPHESIANS 4:22-32).

It is vital that you be led by the Spirit in this as in everything. Ask the Lord to show you what new behaviors He wants you to "put on" to replace the sinful activities you once did. Don't try to think up the "right answer" on your own! Wait quietly before the Lord, expecting Him to tell you what He wants you to do. His voice is sensed as flowing thoughts while your heart and inner eyes are focused on Him. He has wonderfully creative ideas that are so much more effective than anything we would come up with on our own. Give Him the chance to give you His instructions for you, personally. Then depend on His strength to obey.

When God has given you His strategy for overcoming the sinful habit, say it out loud. We must both believe in our hearts and confess with our mouths. So lay your hand on your heart and say "Holy Spirit, cut out of my heart any evil desire to (state the ungodly activity) and give me a renewed heart, I pray." (Look to see Jesus doing this. Watch until He is no longer moving.) Then say, *"From this day on, **by the power of the Holy Spirit**, I will* (state the countering godly activity). *Thank You, Lord, for setting me free from this bondage and granting me new life in Christ. I receive it with joy!"*

Now take some time to let the Holy Spirit minister to you. Slow down and tune to flowing thoughts, pictures and emotions as you do this so you can experience the spiritual transformation taking place. Watch what Jesus does; listen to what He says; record it so you can meditate on it frequently and return to it when you need strength. Believe that what He has promised to do, He has done. He has set you free!

Repeat this prayer whenever the Spirit shows you a sin He wants to deal with. As you go forward in your walk with the Lord, the Holy Spirit will continue to let you know areas of your life that He wants to change. Don't be discouraged when you see your failings. Be glad that your eyes are opened to the destructive road you were on and that you now have a way to turn around (repent), get off that path and go the right way because of the power of the Spirit within you.

Transformed Into His Image

The Lord's desire for you is that you would be transformed into the image of His Son, Jesus Christ. The more time you spend getting to know Him and meditating on all that He is and looking at Him as in a mirror, recognizing that He is now in you and joined to you, the more you will become like Him (2 Cor. 3:18). If you look at yourself and your weakness and failures and sinfulness, you will remain stuck living like the old man. It is in knowing the truth about who you are and Who Christ is within you that you are set free to be all that you were created to be (Jn. 8:32). When the Son sets you free, you are free indeed (Jn. 8:36)!

Additional Resources

- *Naturally Supernatural*—Mark and Patti Virkler
- *How to Walk by the Spirit*—Mark and Patti Virkler

Personal Application

1. What changes have you seen in your life since you were born again? What sins did the Lord immediately deliver you from?

Have others noticed any changes in you? Praise God for His cleansing!

_____

_____

_____

_____

_____

2. What is God's promise to you in 1 Corinthians 10:13 and 2 Corinthians 12:9?

_____

_____

_____

3. *But we all, with unveiled face, beholding as in a mirror the glory of the Lord, are being transformed into the same image from glory to glory, [which comes from] the Lord, the Spirit.*　　(2 CORINTHIANS 3:18)

In your own words, how does this verse say that you overcome sin and become more like Christ?

_____

_____

_____

4. The next time you are tempted, look to the Spirit within you to overcome. Record your experience.

_____

_____

_____

_____

5. Ask the Lord to show you what new behaviors He wants you to "put on" to replace the sinful activities you once did. Don't try to think up the "right answer" on your own. Wait quietly before the Lord expecting Him to tell you what He wants you to do. His voice is sensed as flowing thoughts while your heart and inner eyes are focused on Him. He has wonderfully creative ideas that are so much more effective than anything we would come up with on our own. Give Him the chance to give you His instructions for you, personally. Record what He says to you, then depend on His strength to obey.

_____

_____

_____

_____

_____

6. Select one of the verses from this chapter to hide in your heart through meditation and memorization.

GROUP ACTIVITIES

1. Share your answers to the questions. Rejoice in the victories; encourage one another; pray for those struggling.

2. Share your memory verses and the reasons why you chose that verse. How has the Lord ministered to you through it?

3. Have a time of journaling together according to the pattern in the Group Activities of Chapter 9.

12

If Anyone Sins

You have embraced Jesus as your Lord and Savior, committing yourself to Him and trusting Him to be the ransom for your sins that brings you God's forgiveness. You have received a new heart and a new spirit, which is joined to the Holy Spirit. With all that is in you, you want to live in a way that will please your new Lord. You want to obey His commands because you love Him and because you recognize that they are the signposts that will lead you into the abundant, joyful and peace-filled life that you long for.

But, what if you fail? What if, when the temptation comes, instead of resisting, you just give in without a fight—or you fight in your own strength and lose? What if you momentarily forget Who is in charge of your life and you retake the throne? What if you sin? Does that mean you weren't really born again?

Absolutely not.

John was one of the twelve disciples who walked with Jesus while He was on earth. In fact, John was one of Jesus' closest friends. Later in his life, he wrote the Gospel of John, as well as some letters to individual believers and churches. That is important to notice:

his letters were written to believers, people like you who were born again. Look at what he has to say in his first letter:

> *If we claim to be without sin, we deceive ourselves and the truth is not in us. If we confess our sins, he is faithful and just and will forgive us our sins and purify us from all unrighteousness. If we claim we have not sinned, we make him out to be a liar and his word is not in us. My dear children, I write this to you so that you will not sin. But if anybody does sin, we have an advocate with the Father—Jesus Christ, the Righteous One. He is the atoning sacrifice for our sins, and not only for ours but also for the sins of the whole world.*

(1 JN. 1:8-10, 2:1, 2)

So while it is not God's best for you if you sin, you do not take Him by surprise when you do. He understands our weakness and has made preparations in advance for when we fall.

WHat DOESN'T HAPPEN

First, let's take a look at what does not happen when you sin.

You do not lose your salvation. All is not lost. You are still a child of God. If you choose to continue to live a sinful life, preferring not to bow before Jesus as your Lord, you may not have really been born again in the first place. But if, when you sin, your heart is grieved and you wish you hadn't done it, that means the Holy Spirit is still within you convincing you of your sin and calling you to repentance.

God does not stop loving you. God is crazy about you! There is absolutely no bad thing you can do that will make Him love you any less, or any good thing you can do that will make Him love you any more. He loves you with an everlasting love.

He is not mad at you when you fail and He does not turn away from you. You may be tempted to turn from Him, but He will never turn away from you or reject you. He adores you!

God does not punish you. Jesus is your Savior. He has taken the punishment for all your sins—those you committed in the past, those you may be committing now, and any you may commit in the future. Jesus is the atoning sacrifice, the ransom, the payment for every sin you ever commit. The punishment for your sins was placed on Jesus at the cross and He paid the price. There is no condemnation, no penalty, no punishment for those who are in Christ Jesus, and that is you (Rom. 8:1).

WHat Does Happen

If God doesn't get mad at you or punish you, then why bother to resist temptation? Why not just go ahead and enjoy the pleasures of sin? *May it never be! How shall we who died to sin still live in it?* (Rom. 6:2).

So what does happen when you sin?

You lose your peace. One of the most precious blessings of salvation is the peace of God that fills our hearts when we have been born again. Our hearts are clean and our spirits feel light. The burden of our sin and our ungodly lifestyles is lifted off our shoulders. Peace flows within like a river. But when you disobey your Lord, you lose that peace. It feels like being born again backwards. Those old feelings of guilt, worthlessness and shame sneak back into your mind. Your spirit knows that you are not in perfect unity with your Father. Your conscience accuses you. The Holy Spirit within convicts you, calling you to confess, to change direction and to turn back to the Father.

Your close relationship with God may suffer—not because He has withdrawn but because you do. When you know you have sinned, you may be tempted to avoid the Lord so you stop journaling, reading your Bible or having quiet times with Him. You may project your anger at yourself onto Him and assume that because you are disappointed in yourself, He is also disappointed with you. Like Adam and Eve in the Garden, you may try to hide from Him because of your feelings of guilt and shame.

You miss out on some of God's blessings. It's not that He's withheld the blessing from you. Instead, you have not positioned yourself to receive it from Him. You have stepped out from under God's waterfall of blessings. Some things God tells us to do because they release His blessing into our lives. For example, He says, "Honor your father and mother, that it may go well with you and that you may live long on the earth" (Eph. 6:2, 3).

There are many reasons why honoring your parents improves the quality of your life, such as the Law of Sowing and Reaping and the Law of the Harvest. The Law of Sowing and Reaping says that whatever you sow is what you reap. Whatever you "plant" in life is what you will receive back. If you sow love, you reap love. If you sow honor, you reap honor. If you sow disrespect, you reap disrespect. If you sow anger, you reap anger.

The Law of the Harvest, also known as the Law of Increase, says that you don't just reap the same amount as you sow; the harvest is exponentially larger than the seed. If you sow a kernel of corn, you don't reap one kernel. Why bother to plant it if you are just going to get the same thing back? No, you reap several ears of corn and multiplied kernels. If you sow an apple seed, you do not reap one apple; you reap a tree that bears fruit for years. The Bible says it this way: "They sow the wind and reap the whirlwind" (Hos. 8:7).

So one way your life goes better if you honor your parents is that you will reap even greater honor from your children than you give to your parents. I don't know how honoring your parents extends the years of your life, but since God said it, it must be true.

Finances are another area where obedience results in increased blessings. *"Whoever is generous to the poor lends to the LORD, and he will repay him for his deed"* (Prov. 19:17 ESV). *"Those who give to the poor will lack nothing, but those who close their eyes to them receive many curses"* (Prov. 28:27). *"Give, and it will be given to you. A good measure, pressed down, shaken together, and running over will be poured into your lap. For with the measure you use, it will be measured back to you"* (Lk. 6:38). *"Consider this: Whoever sows sparingly will also reap sparingly, and whoever sows generously will also reap generously* (2 Cor. 9:6). When we are generous to the poor, the Lord repays us even more generously. If we do not give to the poor, we don't receive that blessing.

Since the time of the Father of our Faith, Abraham, in the book of Genesis, tithing or returning one-tenth of your income to God, has been a way of recognizing His Lordship in your life and the fact that it is by His strength that you are able to earn anything. We are only stewards of our possessions, and tithing reminds us that it all belongs to God.

But with the law of tithing comes an amazing promise: *"'Bring the whole tithe into the storehouse, so that there may be food in My house, and test Me now in this,' says the LORD of hosts, 'if I will not open for you the windows of heaven and pour out for you a blessing until it overflows'"* (Mal. 3:10). Failing to pay your tithe prevents that blessing from pouring into your life.

We miss out on many of God's choicest blessings when we fail to walk in obedience to Him.

There are natural consequences of your sin, interfering with the abundant life God wants to give you. Suddenly things aren't going as well for you as they were. God's rules are for your good, because He knows the results of living contrary to them. Relationships might be challenged, your job may be in jeopardy, you may even face legal consequences. These are not God's punishments; they are the expected outcomes of your own choices.

We don't need to know what the consequences of breaking one of His laws will be before we decide if we will obey it. It is enough to know that He loves us and wants to bless us. If we tell our children not to play in the street, they don't need to know that a body in motion tends to stay in motion, or the formula to determine the stopping distance of a moving object based on speed and weight, or the result of large vehicles intersecting with small bodies. They just need to know that we love them and want to protect them, and one of the rules for their protection is to stay out of the street. In the same way, we don't need to fully understand all of God's reasons for the commands He gives us before we obey Him. It is enough to know that He loves us and is trying to protect us, and disobeying Him has consequences that we want to avoid.

These are not God punishing you; they are the natural outcomes that God knew would follow certain behaviors so He warned you against them. They are what happens when you step out of an airplane without a parachute. If you put your hand on a hot stove, you get burned, not as punishment but just because that's the way it is. We talked about some of these earlier. If you lie to your spouse, he or she will lose their trust in you and your relationship will be weakened. If you spend all your money supporting your addiction to alcohol, drugs, gambling, or anything else, your financial situation will quickly deteriorate. If you commit immorality, your heart will (eventually) be broken, other relationships will be fractured, and you may contract diseases.

If you are an angry, unforgiving grouch, you will have problems at work and at home. Toxins will be released in your body that will cause pain in your joints and possibly diseases in your organs. You will be as miserable as you are making everyone else.

Sin brings unhappiness, brokenness, lack, sickness and pain.

WHaC Can I DO?

Let's go back to First John:

> If we confess our sins, he is faithful and just and will forgive us our sins, and purify us from all unrighteousness. My dear children, I write this to you so that you will not sin. But if anybody does sin, we have an advocate with the Father—Jesus Christ, the Righteous One. He is the atoning sacrifice for our sins, and not only for ours but also for the sins of the whole world. (1 JN. 1:9, 2:1,2 NIV)

God has promised that if we will confess our sins to Him, He will forgive us and cleanse us because of the sacrifice of Jesus Christ. So when you sin, run to Him right away for help. Don't wallow in guilt, moaning that your sin is so bad that you cannot possibly be forgiven. Can any sin be bigger than Christ's ransom? Don't waste time trying to avoid God or His people, thinking they won't want you around anymore. Is any sin greater than God's love?

Don't try to clean yourself up by "doing better" before you present yourself to God. Don't perform acts of penance or extra good deeds to try to make God like you again. Just run to Him! He knows what you did and He still loves you. He wants to forgive you. Jesus died a horrible death for your cleansing. Don't dishonor His incredible sacrifice by rejecting the forgiveness He is offering you.

So, if you sin, immediately go to God and tell Him what you did. Repent, turn away from your sin and turn back to the Lord. Remember His promise: *"If we confess our sins, He is faithful and righteous to forgive us our sins and to cleanse us from all unrighteousness"* (1 Jn. 1:7-9). *"Repent, then, and turn to God, so that your sins may be wiped out..."* (Acts 3:19). *"Turn to the Lord...for He will freely pardon"* (Isa. 55:7).

Speak it: "Lord, I am sorry for committing this sin of _____. I turn away from ___ (list sin) and I turn to You, Jesus, receiving Your blood which is washing over it and cleansing me of the guilt of this sin and making me totally clean. Jesus, You are my Lord, my Ruler, my Commander. I do want You to be on the throne of my life. Please take Your place there once more. Thank You for Your mercy, Your faithfulness and Your righteousness that forgives me and cleanses me completely."

See it: See yourself handing the sin to Jesus, Jesus taking it, washing it away and cleansing you. See Jesus giving you a garment of white to wear, which is His righteousness (Gal. 3:27). You stand complete in Him (Col. 1:28). You have put on His righteousness, just as a woman on her wedding day puts on a beautiful gown of white. You stand spotless, glowing, radiating His glory.

Let the Holy Spirit minister: Slow down this process. Don't rush. Take your time. As you see yourself handing the sin to Jesus and watch Him take it and cleanse you, tune to flow, and let that picture come alive by the life of the Holy Spirit. Watch the flowing picture as Jesus interacts with you.

sanctified

We know that anyone who has been born of God does not keep on sinning (1 Jn. 5:18), but if we sin, Jesus is still our Savior Who forgives and cleanses.

Putting off the sins that trip you up is the process of sanctification, of working out your salvation, for it is God Who is producing in you both the desire and the ability to do what pleases Him (Phil. 2:12,13). As you submit to Him and look into His face, He will transform you daily into the image of His dear Son (Rom. 8:29).

And never, ever give up! It is God who as work in you, and He will be with you until the end. You can be "confident of this, that He who began a good work in you will carry it on to completion until the day of Christ Jesus" (Phil. 1:6 NIV). He will finish what He started in you!

PErsonal application

1. Read Romans 8:1 and ask the Lord to talk to you about what it means to you personally.

    _____

    _____

    _____

2. Has there been an occasion when you have sinned since becoming a believer? What were the results in your life? How did you feel? What did you do to restore your relationship with the Lord?

_____

_____

_____

_____

_____

3. Carefully read the promises concerning giving and tithing that are quoted in the chapter, asking the Holy Spirit to show you how He wants you to apply those truths in your life. Record what He says to you.

_____

_____

_____

4. Select one of the verses from this chapter to hide in your heart through meditation and memorization.

GROUP ACTIVITIES

1. Share your answers to the questions.

2. Share your memory verses and the reasons why you chose that verse. How has the Lord ministered to you through it?

3. Have a time of journaling together according to the pattern in the Group Activities of Chapter 9.

13

Renew Your Mind

The great purpose for which you were born again was that you might become like Jesus Christ. Everything the Spirit does in you and for you and through you is to make you into His image and likeness. You are meant to be conformed to the image of Jesus, the Son of God, so that He might be the firstborn among many brothers and sisters (Rom. 8:29). What an amazing destiny!

God doesn't want you to simply try to act the way you think Jesus acted. He doesn't want you to merely look like Jesus on the outside, even if you could. No, Christianity is an inside job. God is more concerned about the condition of your heart and mind and spirit than about your behavior. He wants any change in you to be worked from the inside out, not imposed from the outside.

Integral to that process is renewing your mind (Rom. 12:2). Remember, "to repent" means "to change your mind." Your thoughts and attitudes and beliefs have been primarily formed by your environment—your family, social network, schools, and media. Unfortunately, those influences are largely contrary to the ways of God, so your thinking is contrary to the ways of God. You must repent, change your mind, and learn to listen to the Spirit within you to direct your thoughts.

YOU HAVE AN ENEMY

You may not have been aware of it, but you are involved in a war. There is a very real enemy who was not happy when you made your commitment to the Lordship of Jesus Christ. The devil is real and his demons are real, and they are your enemies. They will do everything in their power to steal every blessing the Lord wants to give you and destroy all that is good in your life (Jn. 10:10). But praise God, they don't have very much power any more. Jesus' death and resurrection broke the power and authority of the devil and totally defeated him. Jesus has won the victory! The only weapon the devil has left is deception. He is the father of lies and he uses his weapon effectively against anyone who is not on guard against him.

Yes, Jesus won the victory and Satan is defeated. But he has not accepted his loss, so it is our responsibility to enforce Jesus' victory. Jesus has given us authority over the enemy so we need not have any fear of him (Lk. 10:19). Satan must accede to our dominion over him in Jesus' Name.

Abraham Lincoln authorized the Emancipation Proclamation which freed every slave in the United States from their bondage. He had the authority to do so and the power of the government to enforce his decree. And every slave that heard the word and believed it was legally empowered to walk away from his "owner." Yet there were some slaves who did not immediately go free. Some never heard the Proclamation. Others heard but were convinced by their masters that it did not apply to them. So though they were legally free, they continued to live as slaves.

It is the same way for us. Jesus has purchased our freedom, but we must believe it and walk in it. We must do the "mop up" work of the war, imposing His victory on the enemy and making sure he doesn't hold any ground in our lives.

Take Every Thought Captive

Thankfully, as we said, the only power Satan has left is the power to deceive, but you have the Truth. Just as light must always overcome darkness, so the Truth will always overcome a lie. In the same way that the Lord's voice comes to you as spontaneous thoughts, so does the devil try to fill your mind with his lies. But you don't have to put up with any of it!

> *For though we walk in the flesh, we do not war according to the flesh, for the weapons of our warfare are not of the flesh, but divinely powerful for the destruction of fortresses. We are destroying speculations and every lofty thing raised up against the knowledge of God, and we are taking every thought captive to the obedience of Christ* (2 COR. 10:3-5).

You have been given the power and authority to destroy every lie that Satan throws your way. You have the Truth, for Jesus is the Truth. But it is your responsibility to take every thought captive to the obedience of Christ. Your mind is the battleground of the war.

You must not allow any thought to remain in your mind that is contrary to the truth of God's word. Do not accept any thought about yourself that God doesn't have about you. Do not meditate on any picture that does not have Jesus in it. Take authority over your own mind and don't let the enemy harass or defeat you any longer.

Ask the Holy Spirit to begin right now making you more aware of the thoughts that fill your mind. Ask Him to show you the lies and begin replacing them with the truth. For example, late one night you may begin to think, "Nobody cares about me. I am all alone. If I died right now, no one would even care." As soon as you are aware of that thought, stop it in its tracks with the truth. "Satan, that is a lie! I am not alone. God has promised He will never leave me or forsake me. He loves me with an everlasting love. He loved me so much that Jesus died for me. I reject that lie and command you to be quiet and leave me alone!"

If you can say it aloud, do so, with force and authority. If you must whisper it, it can still be with authority. And he must obey you (Jas. 4:7). Then begin to fill your mind with the truth. Remember the things the Lord has done for you, the blessings He has given you, the love He has expressed to you. Call to mind words from your journaling in which the Lord told you how special you are to Him and meditate on them. Truth is the weapon of our warfare that destroys, tears down and takes captive every lie of the enemy.

The devil is very sneaky and very nasty, and he has ways of inserting his lies into our hearts and minds without our even being aware of it. We're going to expose some of his tactics so that he can no longer use them against you. The greater knowledge and awareness you have of the enemy's ways, the more effective your warfare against him will be, and the more you will walk in victory.

THE LIES WE BELIEVE

Did you have a nickname when you were young? Did one of your physical characteristics become your entire identity when you heard Fatso, Beak, Beanpole, Four-Eyes, Miss Piggy or some other cruel name? Were your parents or teachers impatient with your weaknesses, so they tried to shame them out of you with words like Dummy, Sissy, Cry Baby, Moron, Idiot, Loser or Jerk? Was your religion or ethnicity different from your companions so they gave you a derogatory label?

Whoever said, "Sticks and stones may break my bones but names will never hurt me" was very much mistaken. Names hurt—a lot—with a pain that can last throughout our lives. They become the lens through which we see ourselves so that we never have a clear, true vision of who we are.

We had a friend who was called "Fatty" by her brothers when she was a child. By the time she was a teenager, she suffered from bulimia. When we met her in her twenties, she had lost all of her teeth—destroyed by the self-induced vomiting. The lies we believe shape our lives.

Maybe you weren't tormented by any particular nickname but you suffered the emotional abuse of constant criticism, derision or mockery. If you spilled the milk at the dinner table, did you hear, "You clumsy oaf! What is wrong with you? You're not fit to eat at the table with civilized people." If you didn't earn 100% on a test, were you treated like a failure? When you weren't athletic like your father but instead preferred more cerebral activities, did he make you feel like you were a disappointment? Those kinds of experiences hardwire our brains to believe that we are less than we are, that we are unworthy, unloved, and hopeless. These are the lies that Jesus wants to clear from our hearts and minds.

WORD CURSES

Do any of these sound familiar?

"You'll never make it!"

"You are such a loser!"

"You'll never amount to anything!"

"How can you be so stupid?"

"You are totally tone-deaf!"

"You have two left feet!"

"You are so dense!"

"What a wimp!"

"You're hopeless!"

"He's the dumb jock."

"This is the computer nerd."

"She's the 'blonde' in the family, if you know what I mean."

Just as God created the world by the words that He spoke, He has given us the power to create with our words. The words that were spoken over you as a child carried a creative energy that produced the reality that was spoken. Now, as an adult, you may feel trapped in patterns of behavior that you recognize are destructive but from which you seem unable to break free. You carry beliefs about yourself that are totally contrary to who you are capable of being. These thought and behavior patterns can be traced directly back to words spoken by your parents or teachers when you were a child. They have cut into your heart like arrows where the poisonous tips have remained to infect your spirit.

Words spoken over you by yourself or by others are powerful and release spiritual forces which lead toward life or death. Word curses add negative spiritual energy to our lives that create invisible barriers which keep us from experiencing God's blessing.

"There is one who speaks rashly like the thrusts of a sword, but the tongue of the wise brings healing."

(PROVERBS 12:18 NASU)

"A soothing tongue is a tree of life, but perversion [viciousness] in it crushes the spirit." (PROVERBS 15:4 NASU)

"Death and life are in the power of the tongue..."

(PROVERBS 18:21 NASU)

Ask the Lord what word curses you have spoken over yourself or others have spoken over you, which are lies that the enemy has been using to keep you from being all God intends for you to be. Then break the power of those words in prayer:

- I **confess** and repent for receiving the word curse stating that "I _____", and for any anger or resentment against You, God, for allowing this to happen in my life.

- I **forgive and release** _____ (self & others) for speaking this over me. I ask You, God, to forgive me, and I receive Your forgiveness. I forgive myself for participating in this sin.

- I **joyfully accept** the divine exchange Christ made for me on the cross of Calvary. I break this curse over me right now in the name of the Lord Jesus Christ and I receive His divine blessing of _____ (the opposite) which replaces this curse.

Be sure to listen for the truth that God wants to speak to you to replace the lie that you have believed. Ask Him to show you yourself as He sees you. Then fill your mind with God's words and vision. Meditate on His truth for you whenever you get a chance. Shine the light of truth into your heart and mind to drive out the darkness of Satan's lies.

NeGative expectations

A negative expectation is a damaging belief system which has been established in your heart somewhere along the road of life. Negative expectations can be against yourself, others, authorities, institutions, or even God. Most of these are on the unconscious level, so we are generally not even aware that we are holding them. But if we want to be like Jesus, we must repent of them and change our minds, embracing and believing the truth.

Negative expectations can come from word curses spoken over you or word curses you speak over yourself. Someone may tell you that you are stupid which produces a negative expectation that you will act as if you are stupid. I used to speak word curses over myself. I said things like, "I am a 'B' level student. The alphabet and I don't get along well together. I can't spell." Each of these produced negative expectations and set negative forces alive within me, releasing the fulfillment of my words.

Negative expectations may come from your heart digesting a hurtful experience and then creating a belief based on the experience. For example, if you say something and are ridiculed or punished for it, you could begin to believe the lie that, "If I express my opinion, I will be rejected." If your parents had a poor marriage, you may believe that "All men are workaholics" or "All women are unfaithful." The list of possible negative expectations is endless.

Often these expectations are self-reinforcing, for whatever you expect and believe will happen, most likely will happen (Matt. 9:29). It is important that you examine the conscious and unconscious beliefs and judgments you hold, and ensure that they all line up with the Bible. Those that don't will need to be repented of and renounced and replaced with a more biblical belief system.

But in order to replace your negative beliefs, you need more than a "one-liner" from the Bible that states an opposite to your old belief system. It is not enough for your brain to memorize a new verse which counters the negative belief you were holding. You need more than a new verse; you need a new faith. Faith is born in revelation, when God speaks into your heart enlightening you to new insights from the Holy Scripture.

Memorizing a new verse can assist in the birthing of a new faith within your heart, but, technically speaking, faith doesn't come from your memorizing a verse of Scripture. Nor does faith come through the persuasive words of wisdom given by a counselor (1 Cor. 2:4-5). Faith comes by hearing the word of God (Rom. 10:17). In the original Greek, "word" is *rhema*, and it means "spoken word." Faith comes from the spoken word of God.

Specifically, faith comes when the Holy Spirit speaks a word into your spirit, or when the Holy Spirit illuminates a verse of Scripture, making that verse leap off the page and into your heart. Then you know in your spirit that God is giving that verse to you for the situation you are facing. God's faith is a result of receiving God's revelation.

I have heard counselees say by rote a verse that I have told them to confess, and yet I am fully aware that they do not believe in their heart the words they are declaring. They have not mixed faith with the words they have heard (Heb. 4:2). Instead, they are still believing the contradictory negative thought—the lie—which brought them into my office in the first place. Saying a verse does not mean you have revelation concerning that verse in your heart. It is the revelation of God in your heart that changes your heart, not the words you parrot with your mouth.

So once God has made you aware of a negative expectation that you are holding, ask Him to show you His truth to replace it. Take time to journal, hear His voice and see His vision. Spend time meditating on the Scriptures. Let revelation birth faith in your heart, and when you **know** the truth, get rid of the lie through prayer:

- I **confess** and repent of believing the lie that _____ and for the ways I have judged others and/or institutions based upon this negative belief.

- I **forgive** _____ for contributing to my forming this negative expectation/belief. I ask You to forgive me, and I receive Your forgiveness. I forgive myself for believing this lie.

- I confess the countering divine truth that _____ .

Spend time meditating and pondering God's truth. Fill your mind with light so there is no room for darkness.

Inner vows

Inner vows are the promises or statements you make as a result of the negative expectations that you hold. Inner vows are usually on the unconscious level, and correspond to the negative expectations you have. For example:

The negative expectation *"I believe/expect ..."*	The resulting inner vow *"Therefore ..."*
I'll probably fail.	I won't try.
Most marriages fail.	I won't give myself totally to my spouse.
Nobody likes me.	I will be unfriendly first.
I'm ugly.	I will hide myself.

The negative expectation	The resulting inner vow
"I believe/expect ..."	*"Therefore ..."*
I'm dumb.	I won't do my best.
I'm fat.	I will just be a couch potato.
I'm no good.	I will act out my evil impulses.
I don't deserve a good life.	I won't try to improve my life.
I will never be out of debt.	I won't try to excel financially.
I don't deserve God's blessing.	I will make it on my own.
My sin is unforgivable.	I will hide from God.
My children will rebel.	I will control them.
Life is unfair.	I will distrust and withdraw.
Satan is powerful.	I will try not to attract his attention.
People don't accept me.	I will put up a protective wall.
I must be perfect.	I will try hard.
Men don't cry.	I will stuff my emotions.
If I'm transparent I'll be hurt.	I will hide my weaknesses.
All politicians are evil.	I will never trust a politician.
The government is out to get me.	I will prepare for siege.
Godly businessmen can't succeed.	I will compromise my integrity.

Whatever you have expected and vowed to get, you will receive. It is that simple. You receive exactly what you believe for and exactly what you have promised yourself (Matt. 9:29). If you promise yourself failure, you will fail. If you promise yourself destruction at the hands of an evil government, you will be destroyed at the hands of an evil government. Look at this amazing verse from the Old Testament:

How long shall I bear with this evil congregation, which murmur against me? I have heard the murmurings of the children of Israel, which they murmur against me. Say unto *them, "As truly as I live," saith the LORD, "**as ye have spoken in mine ears, so will I do to you**."*   (NUMBERS 14:27-28)

The Israelites had confessed over and over that they were going to die in the wilderness. They expected to die. They said they would die, and sure enough, God said, "I am going to give you exactly what you have been believing for and confessing. You will die in the wilderness."

This actually countered God's plan for their lives, for God had intended to give them the Promised Land. But their negative expectations and inner vows and negative confession brought them destruction rather than God's plan of Promised Land blessings. What a sobering truth for our own lives. We can miss God's choice blessings for our lives by believing for and confessing demonic negatives rather than Holy Spirit positives.

Of course, you realize immediately that this works just as well, if not better, in the positive. If you expect God's promises of blessing and provision and His watchful care over you, you will receive them, also. According to your faith it will be done to you, and what you say, you get. So spend some time with the Lord, asking the Holy Spirit to show you any inner vows you have made that are controlling your behavior and preventing the full expression of the new life He has given you. Overcome through the power of the Spirit within you.

THE ACCUSER

The essence of Satan's nature is to accuse. The Greek word *diablos*, which is translated "devil," literally means "accuser" or "slanderer." The central work of Satan is to accuse day and night.

In Revelation we read, "And I heard a loud voice in heaven, saying, 'Now **the salvation**, and **the power** and **the kingdom of our God** and **the authority of His Christ** have come, for the accuser of our brethren has been thrown down, who accuses them before our God day and night.'" (Rev. 12:10, 11). Notice that salvation, power, the kingdom of God and the authority of Christ come in our lives when we overcome and cast down the accuser.

If the essence of Satan's character is to accuse, whom then does he spend his time accusing? First, as we see here in Revelation, he accuses the brethren to God. In Job 1:9, Satan is accusing Job's motives before God: "Does Job fear God for no reason?" In other words, "Of course Job fears You and serves You, God. Look at all the blessings You have lavished upon him. He only serves You out of selfishness. He doesn't really love You, only the things You give him."

The accusation of the brethren is not limited to the throne room of God. Every negative evaluation, every critical judgment, every accusing thought against another which finds its way into our minds has as its source the accuser of the brethren. When we cooperate with his evil purposes and speak forth words of accusation against the brethren, our tongues are "set on fire by hell" (Jas. 3:6). When our hearts are filled with demonic wisdom, jealousy, selfish ambition, disorder and every evil thing find a comfortable home (Jas. 3:15,16).

Satan also accuses us personally, challenging, criticizing and condemning us in our own eyes. When the Holy Spirit led Jesus into the wilderness, Satan met Him there and said, "*If* You are the Son of God..." (Lk. 4:3). Can you hear the accusation in those words? "*If* You are really who You say You are...." He will do the same thing to you: "*If* you really are a child of God, why do you act the way you do? If you're so spiritual, why don't you pray more? If you were a good Christian, you would read your Bible more. You wouldn't get mad so often. You wouldn't do this. You would do that." On and on the accusations mount in your mind until you accept the judgment as valid and give up in despair.

Satan even accuses God to us. Remember, in the Garden of Eden, Satan (the serpent) said to the woman, "Indeed, has God said, 'You shall not eat from any tree of the garden?' ...For God knows that in the day you eat from it your eyes will be opened, and you will be like God, knowing good and evil'" (Gen. 3:1,5). Can you hear him challenging the motivation of God, accusing God of selfishly trying to keep something good to Himself? Particularly when we are already tending toward depression and self-pity, this is an arrow which easily finds its target in our hearts. "Has God really said that He loves you? If God really loved you, He wouldn't let such terrible things happen to you. If God wanted to, He could stop those people from slandering you like that. If God loved you as much as He loves other people, He'd give you a better job, a nicer house, a happier marriage. God doesn't really love you at all." If you accept these accusations, if you do not challenge their source and their validity, you are on the path to defeat, as surely as Eve was.

Ask the Lord to make you immediately aware when your thoughts are accusing someone—yourself, another person or God. Take authority over that spirit that is trying to contaminate your mind and bring division and command it to be silent. Speak aloud and with authority: "Satan, I reject that accusation and I reject you. I refuse to give you place in my mind. I am a child of God and the Spirit of Christ lives within me. I resist you and command you to be silent and to leave me alone right now. Be gone, in the Name of Jesus Christ!"

Then quiet yourself before the Lord and ask for His truth to fill your heart and mind about the situation. Embrace what He says and meditate on it. Ponder the vision He shows you, and leave no room in your mind for the enemy.

Always on Your Mind

We have already talked about using the eyes of your heart to see Jesus with you when you are spending quiet time with Him. But He is with you all the time, not just when you settle yourself down to hear from Him. The more you develop the habit of recognizing that He is right there with you all the time, the more you will be conformed to His image.

The Bible makes an amazing statement: God will keep you in perfect peace if you keep your mind steadfast and stayed on Him, because you trust in Him (Is. 26:3). The word here for "mind" is translated other places as "imagination," so God wants you to keep your imagination steadfastly focused on Him. If you do, you will trust in Him and He will keep you in perfect peace.

As you go through your day, whatever is happening, look to the Spirit world and remember He is there with you. When you are angry, frustrated, frightened, stressed, worried, anxious, irritated or bored, remember! Take a moment to say, "Lord, let me see You! I know You are here with me. Open my eyes to see what You are doing right here, right now. Let me hear You." When you are excited, happy, grateful, hopeful, inspired or content, remember! Take a moment to say, "Lord, let me see You! I know You are here with me. Open my eyes to see what You are doing right here, right now. Let me hear You."

Keeping the Lord always before you, knowing that He is always with you no matter what you are experiencing, will change the way you live. Taking just a quick moment to look to see what He is doing and listen to hear what He is saying will help transform you into the image of His dear Son. As you see Him in your life, in every situation, you will grow in your trust of Him and He will keep your heart in perfect peace.

prove GOD'S WILL

Do not be conformed to this world, but be transformed by the renewing of your mind, so that you may prove what the will of God is, that which is good and [well-pleasing] and perfect.

(ROM. 12:2)

God's desire for you is an abundant, uncommon, extraordinary, remarkable life (John 10:10). His will for you is all that is good and well-pleasing and perfect. It is His good pleasure to give you the Kingdom of God, which is righteousness, peace and joy in the Holy Spirit (Lk. 12:32, Rom. 14:17). Sadly, most people don't see Him that way. They think His is a cosmic killjoy who takes pleasure in the misery of mere mortals. It is your joyful responsibility to prove to the world what God's will is really like: that which is good and well-pleasing and perfect. You do that by walking in His will, living it out every day. And you can only do that when you have renewed your mind.

As you begin to think God's thoughts and keep your eyes fixed on Jesus throughout our day, your attitudes will be changed. As you spend time getting to know the Lord and experiencing His great love for you, your behavior will change. And as you change, your life will change. You will experience peace that passes all understanding and joy unspeakable and full of glory.

You will reap the blessings of obedience to God's laws. You will avoid the negative consequences of breaking God's laws. It will go well for you. And you will face difficulties with the grace of knowing His love and His presence with you through whatever happens. Your life will become a testimony of God's goodness and His perfect will.

Additional Resources

- *The Supernatural Power of a Transformed Mind*—Bill Johnson
- *The Lies We Believe*—Dr. Chris Thurman
- *Counseled by God*—Mark and Patti Virkler
- *Prayers that Heal the Heart*—Mark and Patti Virkler

Personal Application

1. Read the following verses, asking the Holy Spirit to speak to you through them:

    John 10:10   Luke 10:19
    2 Corinthians 10:3-5   James 4:7

    What is the enemy's plan and what promise are you given concerning it?

    _____

    _____

    _____

2. Did you have a derogatory nickname when you were younger? If you look at your life now, can you see any ways that nickname has affected you? Even if you don't recognize any consequences of the name-calling, Jesus wants to heal

and release you from their influence. Confess any ways in which you accepted or embraced the nickname and all its connotations, believing they were a true reflection of you. By God's grace, forgive those who called you that name and forgive yourself for accepting it. Ask the Lord to break the power of the name in your life and to release you from its effects. Ask Him to give you a new name that proclaims how He sees you and releases His blessings upon you (Rev. 2:17).

Don't allow the enemy to deceive you into continuing to carry the old destructive words with the idea that they are true so you should believe them. If it is contrary to what God says, it is a lie. Never again allow your mind to think of yourself according to the previous name but only according to your new name.

---

3. Did you recognize any of the word curses mentioned in the chapter, or did they remind you of something that has been said about you? Were you aware of the power of those words to influence your life? Can you now recognize any areas of your life that have been in bondage because of words?

Ask the Lord to reveal any word curses that have been spoken over you, then follow the pattern given in the chapter to break free of the power of each one of them.

_____

_____

_____

4. According to Matthew 9:29, why do negative expectations
    have power?

    _____

    _____

    _____

5. Did the Holy Spirit remind you of any negative expectations
    you are carrying? Be sure to take time to ask Him to reveal any
    ways in which you are putting your faith in anything that is
    contrary to Him and His word. Then follow the pattern given
    in the chapter for overcoming each negative expectation,
    being sure to listen to the voice of the Spirit within you
    throughout.

    _____

    _____

    _____

    _____

6. What inner vows have you made based on your negative
    expectations? Ask the Holy Spirit to search your heart and
    bring to your mind any subconscious vows you have made
    that are contrary to God's loving will for you. Take time to
    let Him speak to you and record your conversations. Record
    His truth that drives out the lies. Record His vision for you
    that overcomes any negative inner vows you have previously
    made.

    _____

_____

_____

_____

_____

7. Do you sometimes look at other people and attribute evil motives to them based on outward appearances? When someone offends or hurts you, do you internally accuse their character, intelligence, godliness or intentions? Do you tend to judge others by standards you have established for yourself or for "Christians" or "good people" or "mature people"? Were you aware that when you embrace such thoughts, you are giving the enemy victory in your mind and heart?

   Ask the Holy Spirit to make you aware of any time you accept the accusation of the devil against anyone else. Ask Him to show you truth and give you the grace to reject the whispers of the enemy and listen only to the Spirit of Truth. Take every thought captive to the obedience of Christ!

_____

_____

_____

_____

8. Have you been a victim of Satan's accusations of you to yourself? Have you questioned your salvation or your spirituality or your commitment to God based on something other than God's promises and instructions to you? When such thoughts come to you, resist them, reject them and replace them with the truths the Holy Spirit has revealed to your heart. This is why time meditating on Scriptures and having conversations

with the Lord through two-way journaling is so important: You must have revelation truth that has been birthed faith in your own heart to overcome the lies of the enemy. You must be filled with light so the darkness can find no place in you.

_____

_____

_____

_____

9. Have you heard Satan's accusations of God in your mind? Have you wondered if He really loves you as much as the Scriptures say He does? Have you looked at your circumstances and questioned why He doesn't intervene the way you think He should? Have you doubted that His promises are really for you, considering what kind of person you are and have been? Those thoughts are attacks from your enemy and you have authority to take them captive, resist them, bind them, and command the enemy to be still and leave you in peace. Then quiet yourself before the Lord and ask for His truth to fill your heart and mind. Embrace what He says and meditate on it. Ponder the vision He shows you, and leave no room in your mind for the enemy.

_____

_____

_____

_____

10. For the next week, practice keeping your imagination stayed on the Lord. Ask the Holy Spirit to remind you, and whenever He does, quickly say, "Lord, let me see you right here, right

now. Let me hear you." Then open the eyes and ears of your heart to perceive the spirit world around you. How does it change your perception of reality?

_____

_____

_____

_____

_____

11. Select one of the verses from this chapter to hide in your heart through meditation and memorization.

GROUP ACTIVITIES

1. Share your answers to the questions. Rejoice in one another's victories. Encourage one another in your weaknesses.

2. Share your memory verses and the reasons why you chose that verse. How has the Lord ministered to you through it?

3. Have a time of journaling together according to the pattern in the Group Activities of Chapter 9.

14

Stubborn Sins

You have come so far and grown so much in your knowledge of God's ways, your love for Him, and your walk of faith! You are growing in your confidence that you are recognizing God's voice as you spend time sharing love with Him every day. You are becoming more assured of His overwhelming love for you as you talk with Him, worship Him, listen to your dreams, and meditate on His words to you in your heart and through the Scriptures. Every day, you are becoming more like your Father as you express His love in all you say and do. You have learned that obeying God is for your benefit, and how to resist temptation and live a holy life by the power of the Holy Spirit. You are becoming more like Jesus every day!

But there may be some areas of your life that you are having a hard time surrendering to the Lordship of Jesus. There might be certain temptations that you just keep giving in to, and habits that you know are wrong but you just can't seem to break. In this chapter, we are going to look at two more effects of Jesus' death and resurrection which, if you will receive them in faith, will give you the added power you need to overcome every sin and enticement of the enemy.

It runs in the Family

Is there a particular sin that you are struggling against that you see in other members of your family? Do you find yourself battling with the same weaknesses and frustrations that plagued their lives? Does a tendency toward addiction "run in your family"? Is there a "character flaw" that keeps showing its ugly face?

Perhaps you are dealing with more than environmental influences and learned behavior. Maybe you are battling something deeper than genetics, and stronger than habits. While society calls you a victim and the Church calls you carnal, while Freud blames your sex drive and anthropologists blame the culture, while psychologists argue about the relative influence of environment and heredity, the Bible talks about generational sins and curses. According to the Word of God, the circumstances that affect your life are directly influenced in the spirit realm by the lifestyle of your parents and ancestors (Ex. 20:5). The sins of previous generations can infect your life, making it harder to overcome them than if they were just your own. And under the Law of God, they can bring curses into your life that will hinder the flow of God's blessings to you.

Jesus has redeemed you from the curse of the law by becoming a curse for you. However, until you personally appropriate that redemption in your own life, the curse still operates. When you personally take the cross of Jesus Christ and place it by faith between you and your ancestors, immediately all those generational sins and curses that have been pouring down upon you and your children come to an abrupt and absolute end. They are absorbed into the cross, for Jesus has already paid the price and suffered the penalty. Their power over you is broken because of your faith in the work of Jesus on the cross.

You can be released from the negative sin energies of your ancestors. You can live a life of freedom from the power of generational curses. You can draw freely from the wells of salvation, for the channels of God's grace can be cleared of every obstruction. Your children can start life with a clean slate, unburdened by the consequences of any sin but their own. All you must do is receive it by faith.

Beginning today, you can be a better person, a better Christian, a better spouse, a better parent. Beginning at this very moment, you can be freed from the power of generational sins and curses that have influenced and harassed you all your life. The words below alone will not bring you freedom. You must speak them from your heart with faith. Read the prayer over carefully first, being sure that you understand and can wholeheartedly affirm every word. Then read it aloud prayerfully, from your heart, using the eyes of your heart to see the spiritual realities of which you speak.

"Lord Jesus Christ, I believe that You are the Son of God and the only way to God; and that You died on the cross for my sins and rose again from the dead.

"I give up all my rebellion and all my sin, and I submit myself to You as my Lord.

"I confess all my sins before You and ask for Your forgiveness— especially any sins that exposed me to a curse. [As the Holy Spirit brings specific sins you have committed to your mind, draw upon His grace to truly repent and turn away from them.] *Release me also from the consequences of my ancestors' sins.*

"By a decision of my will, I forgive all who have harmed me or wronged me—just as I want God to forgive me. In particular, I forgive... [As the Holy Spirit brings the names or faces of people to your mind, draw upon His grace to make a decision to forgive them now.]

"I renounce all contact with anything occult or satanic—if I have any `contact objects,' I commit myself to destroy them. I cancel all Satan's claims against me.

"Lord Jesus, I believe that on the cross You took on Yourself every curse that could ever come upon me. So I ask You now to release me from every curse over my life—in Your name, Lord Jesus Christ!"[1]

"I place the cross of Jesus Christ between my ancestors and myself as a baby in my mother's womb. I command the sins and all accompanying curses from my ancestors to be halted at the cross of Jesus Christ, and for freedom and release to flow down from the cross to that baby in the womb." (God lives in timelessness, so this is not a problem for Him. Use the eyes of your heart to increase your faith; see this spiritual reality happening as you pray.)[2]

"By faith I now receive my release and I thank You for it. Lord, I now open myself to receive Your blessing in every way You want to impart it to me."

Praise the Lord! He has redeemed you from the curse of the law!

1 *Blessing or Curse: You Can Choose* by Derek Prince. Chosen Books, ©1990. p.196
2 *Prayers That Heal the Heart* by Mark Virkler. Bridge-Logos Publishers, ©2000. p.54

Enemy Invaders

Another reason you may be having a hard time gaining victory in an area of your life may be that your actions prior to being born again opened the door for the enemy—demons—to attach themselves to you. Don't panic! We haven't slipped over into some kind of fantasy horror show. As we said before, you have an enemy who is real and who has helpers, and those helpers are known as demons. They promote sickness of soul and body, such as compulsive ungodly thoughts, fears, sins and sickness. Fully one-quarter of Jesus' earthly ministry involved casting out demons, and in the early Church, when people came to Christ it was normal to take them through deliverance even before they were baptized. (*Satan: the early Christian tradition* by Jeffrey Burton Russell. Cornell University Press © 1981 page 101)

Before you came to Christ, you were walking according to the power of Satan and his hosts (Eph. 2:2,3). You probably had certain habitual sins that seemed to be just a part of who you were. You accepted and even embraced them. Seeing how much you loved to do those things that were part of Satan's kingdom, a demon may have come along and attached itself to that part of your personality—your soul or mind.

Or maybe you were involved in some kind of non-Christian religion or in some way offered yourself and your resources to a different god. That "god" was really a demon and he was more than happy to take what you offered. Opening yourself up to the spirit realm outside of the covering of Jesus Christ also opened you up to invasion by the enemy, so if you were involved in any kind of meditation that did not have the Father, Jesus or the Holy Spirit as its focus, you probably need deliverance.

The good news is that because you have been purifying your life through your submission to the Lord and putting off the sins of your past, any demons that have been attached to you are starting to get very uncomfortable! As you have been relying on the Holy Spirit to overcome sins in your life, you have weakened the legal bonds that have allowed the demons access to you. When you are ready to command them to leave, they will be ready to go.

One of my students came to me for counseling. He was filled with the Holy Spirit, an active leader in his church, and totally sold out to the Lord. Yet, he still struggled with an addiction to pornography. He hated it and did everything he knew how to do to overcome it. He repented, fasted, prayed, memorized Scriptures, journaled—applied every spiritual discipline he knew yet he still was under its control. I ministered deliverance to him and several demons were cast out. Immediately he recognized a difference in his life. Before, the pull of pornography was so powerful he felt unable to resist. Now, it was just like every other temptation in his life. He was free to give in or resist by the power of the Spirit, according to his own choice. I continued to check back with him over the years and he remained free. Blessed be our Lord and Savior!

Before you address the demons, you will want to repent of any sins which allow the demon a legal foothold in your life. These sins can include harboring anger, unforgiveness and bitterness toward yourself or anyone else, living with flagrant sins, current or past involvement with idols or false religions, or artifacts from false religions.

Then, if you are ready to be free, speak, out loud, renouncing the demon, and commanding it to go. Set your will against it. Speak with authority: *"You demon of ___* (whatever the controlling sin is, that is what you call the demon), *I come against you in the Name of Jesus Christ. I renounce you and the sin of ___. I repent of ____ and I receive forgiveness and cleansing by the blood of Jesus Christ. I do not want you in my life any longer. I command this demon to leave now in Jesus' name. I am filled with the Holy Spirit of God and there is no place for you in my life. You must go now"* (Lk. 10:17). Often there is a sigh or cough or other slight manifestation as the demon departs. You can repeat this prayer a few times if necessary.

When you are sure it is gone (and you will know), continue to speak aloud: *"Holy Spirit, come and fill this area that was left vacant."* Then go and sin no more, lest you pick up something worse than you were just delivered from (Matt. 12:43-45).

If you feel the demon stirring but not coming out, it is because it still has a legal root that is allowing it to stay. In that case, pray and ask the Lord to show you what the legal anchor is that the demon is hanging on to and then honor the spontaneous thoughts coming back to you, as they are God's voice instructing you as to what more needs to be repented of. Repent and state your intention that, from this day on, by the power of the Spirit you are going to live in righteousness in this area. Tell the demon you reject it and command it to go.

If you don't experience full freedom after addressing the demons yourself, it is wise to seek the help of experienced prayer counselors. Check with your church secretary or counseling department to see if they offer inner healing and deliverance. If not, you can call other churches in your area and ask the secretary if their church offers prayer counselors who minister inner healing and deliverance. When you find one that says yes, ask to make an appointment. Your freedom is at stake. Do whatever is necessary to achieve it.

Free Indeed

Jesus has done everything that is necessary to set you free from every bondage to sin. Step into the freedom He offers you by believing and receiving it by faith. If the Son sets you free, you will be free indeed (Jn. 8:36)!

Additional Resources

- *Prayers that Heal the Heart*—Mark and Patti Virkler
- *The Biblical Guidebook to Deliverance*—Randy Clark
- *How to Cast Out Demons*—Doris Wagner
- *Blessing or Curse: You Can Choose*—Derek Prince
- *Restoring the Foundations*—Chester and Betsy Kylstra
- *Breaking Generational Curses*—Marilyn Hickey

Personal Application

1. If you have not already done so, spend time letting the Holy Spirit reveal any generational sins and curses that have been affecting your life. Pray the prayer in faith concerning each one He reveals to you. Remember to use the eyes of your heart to watch the work of the Lord.

2. Ask the Lord of there are any demons who are keeping you in bondage to sin or sickness. Do what is necessary to gain your

total freedom. You were made to have authority over every spiritual enemy. Don't allow his deception to keep you under his power one day longer.

_____

_____

_____

_____

_____

GROUP ACTIVITIES

1. Pray together as a group to break generational sins and curses. Help each person deepen the reality in their lives by describing what you are seeing in the Spirit world as you pray.

2. Provide an opportunity for deliverance to anyone who requests it.

3. Have a time of journaling together according to the pattern in the Group Activities of Chapter 9.

15

When Troubles Come

God loves you and has a wonderful plan for your life! His desire is that you walk in righteousness, peace and joy in the Holy Spirit. He came into the world to destroy the works of the devil and to give you an amazing, abundant, uncommon, extraordinary, remarkable life. He wants you to prosper and be in good health and find success in whatever you put your hand to. He wants you to live the good life!

But we would be remiss if we let you believe that now that you are a Christian, your life will be perfect, that you will get everything you pray for, that you will never have any problems and that everything will go your way. That might be nice, but it is not reality. God didn't save you to take away all your problems; otherwise He could just take you home to Heaven as soon as you were born again. But that is not His plan. We are in the world but not of it. In the world we will have problems, but we can still rejoice because Jesus has overcome the world and He will give us victory as well (Jn. 16:33).

The Bible says that we shouldn't be taken by surprise when we experience trials, temptations, tribulations and even persecution.

172

*Beloved, do not be surprised at the fiery ordeal among you, which comes upon you for your testing, as though some strange thing were happening to you; but to the degree that you share the sufferings of Christ, **keep on rejoicing**, so that also at the revelation of His glory you may rejoice with exultation*

(1 PET. 4:12, 13).

Consider it all joy, *my brethren, when you encounter various trials, knowing that the testing of your faith produces endurance. And let endurance have its perfect result, so that you may be perfect and complete, lacking in nothing.*

(JAMES 1:2-4)

Did you notice the highlighted words in those verses? We are encouraged to rejoice and be joyful when we encounter trials! Is this some kind of masochistic tendency that Christians are supposed to cultivate? Not at all. We do not rejoice because we are suffering; rather, we rejoice because we know that as we submit ourselves to the Lord and depend on Him to carry us through the hard times, we will grow in grace and become more like Jesus. As we hold onto our faith in His love and goodness toward us, even in the face of circumstances that seem to defy that belief, He will reveal Himself to us and in us and we will grow strong in Him. Just like we strengthen our physical muscles through resistance, so is our faith strengthened when we exercise it even when it is hard.

But why do we have to have problems? They may come as small irritations like someone cutting us off in traffic or overwhelming tragedies like losing someone we love. Knowing how the issue came into our lives and how the Lord wants us to respond to it can make all the difference if we want to handle it with grace and peace, emerging victorious and more like Jesus on the other side.

consequences of my sins

We have already talked about the fact that when we break God's laws, there are consequences. Repenting of our sin does not automatically cancel out those costs. If you have lied to your spouse, the relationship will be damaged and it will take time to rebuild trust. If you stole from your boss, you may lose your job and have a hard time finding a new one. That is not an attack of the enemy nor is it punishment from God. It is a natural consequence of choices you made yourself. If you broke the law of the land, you may spend time in jail. If you let your stomach be your god and you constantly overate unhealthy, unclean foods, your body may be weak, sick or diseased and it will take time to rebuild.

If you have truly repented of your sin and turned from it, very rarely the Lord may sovereignly wipe out the consequences of your sin, but you should not expect Him to do so. Instead, He most likely will want to use the negative results of your actions as an opportunity to work on your heart, teaching you and molding you into His image.

If you are facing problems in your life that are the result of your own sinful choices and actions, repent and spend time talking with Him using two-way journaling. Ask Him how He wants you to be responding to the unhappy circumstances you are in. Ask Him what He wants to change in you through this trying time. Ask Him to show you how He wants you to look when you come out the other side in victory. Submit yourself humbly to Him, ponder His words, meditate on His vision, and allow righteousness to triumph.

CONSEQUENCES OF SOMEONE ELSE'S SIN

Unfortunately, we live in a world full of sinners, and the actions of others affect us. An angry motorist may cut you off. A nasty coworker may make snide remarks about you or dump extra responsibilities on you while taking the credit for your successes. A thief may break into your house or car. You may be married to an unbelieving spouse who gambles away your money until the creditors are knocking on your door. Greedy, arrogant or wicked people in power may draw us into wars where innocence is destroyed, bodies are broken and lives are lost. The sins of other people spill over on us every day.

Can you imagine what it would be like to be so hated by your own brothers that they tried to kill you? At the last minute, they decided it would be better to make some money off you so they sold you into slavery. And then, because of the lies of your owner's wife, you were thrown into prison for a crime you didn't commit! Surely God wouldn't allow that to happen to someone He loved! And if it did happen, you would certainly have a right to be angry and bitter toward God and all the people who had treated you so unfairly, right?

Well, that is exactly what happened to a man named Joseph in the Old Testament (Gen. 37, 39-48). But instead of getting mad at God and deciding that God didn't care about him so he was better off on his own, Joseph submitted himself to God. He was so honorable and dependable in his bondage that, even as a slave and a prisoner, he rose to positions of trust and authority. He remained humble in God's sight, never raging against the injustices he suffered but rather living a life pleasing to the Lord.

And because he stayed true to God, God was able to take those wrongs that had been done to him and turn them around to accomplish His purposes for Joseph. Eventually, Joseph became the second most powerful man in the land of Egypt, and his brothers came under his control. Instead of exacting revenge on them or even demanding an apology from them, he declared, "God sent me here to preserve your lives! Even though you meant evil against me, God meant it for good in order to bring about this present result, to preserve many people alive" (Gen. 45:5, 50:20).

In the same way, God can use the evil intentions of other people to propel you toward your destiny, *if you remain true to Him.* If you moan and complain about how poorly you are treated; if you decide to take revenge against those who misuse you; if you interpret hard times as a sign that God doesn't love you or has abandoned you—you will just struggle along alone, angry and bitter. But if you will hold onto your faith in your God, He can use anything for your benefit.

When the consequences of the sins of other people spill over into your life, that is when you need to run to God for covering, for care and for understanding. He knows what is happening but He wants you to express all your hurt and frustrations and anger to Him. But that's not enough. Once you have poured out your feelings, stop in His presence and wait for His response. Let Him tell you whatever He wants to about the situation. Let Him show it to you from His perspective. Allow Him to use the hard times to mold you into the image of His Son Who, when He was reviled and scorned, did not return the abuse but forgave and submitted Himself to the Father.

You cannot do that on your own; you must trust yourself to the power of the Holy Spirit to make you like Him, to give you even the desire to forgive, and the ability to. Ask Him for His mercy and His grace to change your heart so that you respond the way He wants you to. Keep looking at Him and His words and vision to you, not at the wrongs done to you.

Whatever you do, do NOT keep running the movie of the offense over and over in your mind! That is filling your mind with darkness and not the Light of Jesus Christ. You will never be able to forgive and heal if you are constantly replaying the injury. You must take every thought captive and replay God's vision instead. Only then will you be an overcomer.

Remember, the actions of other people are not your responsibility. You are only answerable to God for your reactions and responses. It doesn't matter how much you are sinned against; God can give you the grace to walk in love if you will only give Him the chance.

YOU MISSED HIS STILL, SMALL VOICE

God has promised that He will guide us throughout our day (Is. 48:17). Unfortunately, sometimes in our preoccupation with life, we miss His spontaneous thoughts that could make our way smoother. For example, while brushing your teeth one morning, you have a thought, "I should take Oak Street to work today." But you think more about it as you dress: "I normally take Maple Street because it is quicker. If I take Oak, I need to leave five minutes earlier. I'll just take Maple."

So off you go to work, following your normal route. But halfway down Maple, a water line has burst and emergency vehicles are blocking traffic. Cars are backed up for blocks and there is no way around. You end up being twenty minutes late for work and missing an important appointment. How do you respond? Do you get mad at God for making you late? Do you blame the devil for harassing you? Do you get angry with yourself for not following through on that spontaneous thought that you now recognize was from the Lord?

None of those responses would be particularly productive, so why not take it as a learning opportunity? The Lord said, "Your ears will hear a word behind you, 'This is the way, walk in it,' whenever you turn to the right or to the left" (Is. 30:21). You just experienced that personally, so now you know what God's voice sounds like even better than you did before. You will be more able to recognize Him in the future so you will be quicker to obey His instructions.

And suppose you had left early and gone down Oak Street. You may never have known about the back-up on Maple so you might never have known how the Lord was protecting you. There have been times I have felt led to go to a certain conference or avoid a certain meeting, and I never learned why. It would be tempting in those times to think, "Well, that was just my imagination. Obviously, God didn't have anything for me there." But I choose not to believe that. I choose to believe that God was leading me and that my obedience either protected me from harm or produced a blessing in my life.

Our friend Diane shared such a story with potentially serious consequences: "My sister and I were on the freeway going to a movie. On the way there, the thought kept coming to me to get off at the next off ramp. I ignored it for a while but it would not go away. Finally, I told my sister that we were going to take a different route to the show and got off the freeway.

"When we got home, my mom rushed to the door and said, "You guys are all right?!" We told her yes, and then asked what was wrong. She said that when we left, she saw us in a terrible car accident. So she started to pray and pray and did not stop until she felt that we were safe. I told her about the impression I had to get off the freeway and when I told her what time that was, we learned it was the exact time she had stopped praying. Coincidence? I don't think so." (Mark and Patti Virkler, *4 Keys to Hearing God's Voice* (Shippensburg, PA: Destiny Image Publishers, 2010), 131-132)

Diane and her mother listened to the Lord's warnings, acted upon them, and were protected from potential tragedy. There have been times I have unfortunately ignored those spontaneous thoughts or talked myself out of following them, and found myself without papers I needed or missing an important connection. Sometimes they are just petty annoyances, but God wants to protect you even from minor problems.

Another friend told us about a time when she ignored the Lord's voice, much to her regret: "It was during the construction of [our church facility] and every evening during the week and all day on Saturdays we would gather as a congregation to do our part in its construction. That Wednesday evening I was late getting to the site and even though it was already 8:00 P.M., and darkness had fallen, I was still eager to get to the site to do my part....

"On arriving, I hurriedly parked my car and noticed that there was a group with a portable light working outside to the front of the building and I all could think to myself was to get to that area as quickly as possible so I could do my part of working with them. I decided not to take the designated route in front of a barrier which had been set up to restrict passage to a certain area, but to proceed behind the barrier which was a short route.

"As I started off, a definite thought came to me very clearly: *Judith, go around to the other side.* But I remember saying to myself, "But this is the shorter route and I'll get there faster." As I continued, another very strong thought came to me, *Judith, go around. Do not go this way,* and I remember replying to myself, "But I can see the light."

"That was the last thing I remember, for it turned out that I stepped into a 15-foot-deep pit that had huge boulders at the bottom. I was covered with dirt and was knocked unconscious....

"As I lay on my hospital bed, the first thing I asked of the Lord was to show me what I had missed and He revealed to me very clearly that I had missed knowing and heeding His voice." (Mark and Patti Virkler, *4 Keys to Hearing God's Voice* (Shippensburg, PA: Destiny Image Publishers, 2010), 130-131)

We have heard many stories of people who "had a feeling" they should not go to work or should go in late to the Twin Towers on September 11, 2001. Others deliberately missed their doomed flights because of dreams, prophetic warnings, or uneasiness in their spirits. Was everyone who would be affected by that day of tragedy warned? We will never know. But those who heeded the Lord's warning were spared.

The life of Jesus Himself was saved because the magi and Joseph both took warnings received in their dreams seriously enough to take action upon awakening.

How much trouble and sorrow could we avoid in our lives if we were more fully attuned to the voice of the Spirit in all the ways that He uses to warn us, and if we responded to His warnings with instant obedience?

GOD IS Protecting YOU

Do you remember that old Garth Brooks song, "Unanswered Prayers"? In it he talks about running into a girl he knew when he was young that he had fervently prayed would become his wife. Now, looking at his life, he says,

"As she walked away and I looked at my wife
Then and there I thanked the good Lord
For the gifts in my life.

Sometimes I thank God for unanswered prayers.
Remember when you're talkin' to the man upstairs
That just because he may not answer doesn't mean he don't care.
Some of God's greatest gifts are unanswered prayers."
("UNANSWERED PRAYERS" BY GARTH BROOKS © 1990)

God sees the end from the beginning. He knows what lies down every path you could choose. He knows which way leads to heartache and which way leads to stagnancy and which way leads to joy and fulfillment. He loves you so much, and He wants you to have an extraordinary life! That means that sometimes He will say "No" to your prayers if He knows that answering them with a "Yes" will not be for your best and greatest good.

Suppose you see your child about to dash into the road in front of a speeding car. You will reach out and grab his arm and yank him back to safety any way you can. You won't be gentle. You won't take time to explain why you need to do it. You will simply do whatever it takes to protect your child.

God is the same way with us. He wants to protect us from bad decisions and potential harm, and sometimes the only way He can do it seems painful to us. We may not understand, and He may not even explain the danger to us. (He doesn't have to explain Himself. He is God. We are not.) Isn't it enough to know that He adores us? Can't we trust Him even when we don't understand what He is doing? Is our faith so weak that we question everything we don't understand?

My thoughts are not your thoughts,
  Nor are your ways My ways," declares the LORD.

"For as the heavens are higher than the earth,
  So are My ways higher than your ways
  And My thoughts than your thoughts.   (IS. 55:8,9)

we may not understand, but we can trust

One of the most painful things we may have to face is the death of someone we love. I do not pretend to understand such loss or have all the answers in such a situation. But I have found comfort in these words from Isaiah:

The righteous perisheth,
And no man layeth it to heart,
And godly men are taken away,
None considering
That the righteous is taken away from the evil to come.
He entereth into peace,
They rest in their beds,
Each one that walketh in his uprightness.

(ISAIAH 57:1, 2 FROM THE JEWISH PUBLICATION SOCIETY'S
       1917 EDITION OF THE HEBREW BIBLE IN ENGLISH)

So while of course we mourn our loss as we face life without the one we love, for their sake, because we love them, we rejoice that they are free from the sorrows and evils of this life and are at peace, at home with the Father. Often, if we ask Him for it, the Lord will give us a vision of our loved one in heaven. Keeping that picture in our minds, rather than any memories of their pain or struggles, will help you walk in victory even in sorrow.

When troubles come your way, don't run away from God. Don't allow the accuser to fill your mind with questions about God's love. Don't demand explanations or justifications. Instead, center down into His presence and soak in His love. Meditate on His words to you and replay the visions He has given you. Keep your mind and your imagination steadfastly fixed on the Lord and your trust will be established and you will walk in perfect peace.

your enemy is prowling

It is also possible that when problems come into your life, they are the work of your enemy, the devil, trying to turn you from your faith. But remember, his greatest weapon against you is deception. He is a liar from the beginning. He will try to convince you of things that are only illusions, not reality. And you have all authority over anything he throws your way (Lk. 10:19). If you submit yourself to God, all you need to do is resist the devil and he will run away from you (Jas. 4:7). Yes, your enemy is real but his power over you is limited and most of your spiritual warfare will be for control of your mind.

it's not about you

Sometimes there is a bigger picture than you can see. Hard as it may be to accept, you are not the center of the universe, and sometimes making things go the way you want them to would wreak havoc on a larger plan of God.

Did you ever watch the old Jim Carrey movie, "Bruce Almighty"? There is a scene where God gives Bruce the power and authority to hear and answer prayers. Believing it would be an expression of love, Bruce just answers "yes" to every request. Chaos ensues. Lives are disrupted. No one ends up happy.

Maybe you are planning to go to the park on Saturday so you pray for sunny skies and no rain. But the farmer whose fields border the park is watching his crop dying in the hot sun and desperately praying for rain so that he will be able to pay his bills, feed his children and not lose his land. Whose prayer should God answer? And if God sends rain, what is your response? "Oh God, if You really loved me, You would have given me sunshine! Why don't You answer my prayers? I guess You don't really care about me at all."

In the book of Job, it says that God sends His wind, rain and lightning wherever He commands it, sometimes for correction, sometimes for His world, and sometimes for lovingkindness (Job 37:12,13). God has an entire universe to govern and control. He oversees every detail, from the birth of suns and the movement of planets down to the death of a small bird and the number of hairs on your head! He oversees it all with love and majesty. When things don't go your way, take a step back and remember that you are not the only person God loves and whose life He is blessing and that even though things aren't going the way you want them to, He can still use the circumstances to bring good to you.

HE IS FAITHFUL

What then shall we say to these things? If God is for us, who is against us? He who did not spare His own Son, but delivered

Him over for us all, how will He not also with Him freely give
us all things?   (ROM. 8:31, 32)

Who will separate us from the love of Christ? Will tribulation,
or distress, or persecution, or famine, or nakedness, or peril,
or sword? But in all these things we overwhelmingly conquer
through Him who loved us. For I am convinced that neither
death, nor life, nor angels, nor principalities, nor things
present, nor things to come, nor powers, nor height, nor
depth, nor any other created thing, will be able to separate
us from the love of God, which is in Christ Jesus our Lord.
                                           (ROM. 8:35,37-39)

Whatever the reason for troubles in your life, your response
should always be the same: run to your God, listen to His voice,
look for His vision, then fill your mind and heart with the light of
His presence. You don't need to know the why's or how's behind
your problems. God's answer is always the same: "Trust Me.
Trust in My love for you. I will never leave you or forsake you.
Allow Me to use this for your good and My glory."

We know that God causes all things to work together for good
to those who love God, to those who are called according to His
purpose. For those whom He foreknew, He also predestined to
become conformed to the image of His Son, so that He would
be the firstborn among many brethren.   (ROM. 8:28,29)

After you have suffered for a little while, the God of all grace,
who called you to His eternal glory in Christ, will Himself
perfect, confirm, strengthen and establish you. To Him be
dominion forever and ever. Amen.   (1 PETER 5:10)

If you will submit yourself to God and His love, He will
take whatever touches you and use it for the supreme good of

conforming you to the image of His Son. That is your highest calling and greatest destiny! That is where you will find joy, peace and overwhelming fulfillment. When you can face any circumstance with a heart filled with faith, joy and peace, that truly is an amazing, uncommon, extraordinary, remarkable life.

Personal Application

1. Are you experiencing any negative consequences of your own poor choices in your life right now? Don't depend on your own discernment; ask the Lord through two-way journaling. Let Him show you how He wants to work the hard times out for your good, by conforming you to the image of His Son.

   _____

   _____

   _____

2. Are you experiencing any negative consequences from other people's sin in your life? Those are times when it is hard to trust God's goodness and Lordship. Only by constant communion with Him will you make it through those trials perfect and complete, lacking nothing. Listen for His words, look for His vision, record them, and hold them always in the forefront of your mind. Take every negative thought captive. Reject every lying, accusing, divisive thought the enemy tries to inject into your mind. Submit yourself to God so He can use this trial to prepare you for and bring you into your destiny.

   _____

   _____

   _____

3. Are you facing a trial in your life right now? How have you been responding to it? Can you hold onto your faith and believe in God's goodness to you through it? Will you go to Him and pour out all that you are feeling and struggling with to Him? Will you listen for His words and look for His vision? Will you ponder them in your heart instead of dwelling on the negatives and planning how you will respond out of yourself?

_____

_____

_____

_____

_____

4. Select one of the verses from this chapter to hide in your heart through meditation and memorization.

GROUP ACTIVITIES

1. Share your answers to the questions. Pray with one another for strength and faith to overcome whatever you are each facing. Encourage one another to love and good works.

2. Share your memory verses and the reasons why you chose that verse. How has the Lord ministered to you through it?

3. Have a time of journaling together according to the pattern in the Group Activities of Chapter 9.

16

To Be Like Him

To be like Jesus—what an amazing concept! Have you begun to understand what that means? You were born again so that people today can see God alive in their world the same way people did when Jesus walked on earth. You are a child of Almighty God! You are right now seated with Christ in heavenly places to rule and reign with Him (Eph. 1:20-23, 2:6)! You have received the Holy Spirit not only to empower you to live a holy life but also to carry on what Jesus started by doing good, destroying the works of the devil and healing all who are oppressed by him (Acts 10:38, 1 Jn. 3:8).

There are a few reasons why we have focused up until now on tapping into the power of the Holy Spirit to live a holy life. First of all, it is because that is the harder part. It takes consistent practice to train your senses to distinguish between good and evil (Heb. 5:14). Only time spent in conversations with Jesus will convince you of His love for you, build your trust in Him, and teach you how to walk in love. Learning to recognize the voice of His Spirit within you and respond immediately to His leading prepares you to release His power through you as well.

Another reason we spent so much time on walking in love is because that is the core value of the Kingdom of God. Everything we do flows out of love because everything Christ does flows out of love (Matt. 9:36). If we try to move in the power of God without walking in the love and compassion of God, we will fail. But when we see through God's eyes and hear His voice of love, the Spirit of power can extend out through us and release the Kingdom of God into our world.

YOU WILL BE MY WITNESSES

The last thing Jesus said to His disciples before He was taken up into Heaven was, "Don't do anything until you receive the gift of the Holy Spirit. But when He comes on you, you will receive power and you will be able to see what I am continuing to do here in Jerusalem, throughout the lands of Judea and Samaria, and even to the ends of the earth! Just as I only did what I saw My Father doing and only said what I heard My Father saying, you will be My witnesses who see what I am doing in the spirit and do the same thing in the physical world. You will hear what I am saying and speak that to the people" (see Acts 1:4, 8; Jn. 5:19, 12:49, 50 author's paraphrase).

You have received the gift of the Holy Spirit, if you have asked for the baptism in the Holy Spirit. That means that you are now empowered to carry on the work that Jesus began of sharing the good news of the Kingdom of God and setting the captives free.

The good news of the Kingdom is all that we have been talking about in this book:

- that God loves you with an everlasting love;
- that His Son Jesus died and rose again to take the punishment of our sins;

- that the power of sin and the devil are broken and we can walk in freedom;
- that we can all now talk with God and get to know Him as our Father and personal Friend;
- that by the broken body of Jesus we can be healed of all our sickness and disease;
- that demons must release their hold on us through the power of Jesus' Name;
- that God wants to give us an abundant, extraordinary, uncommon, remarkable life!

It is your great privilege to tell everyone who will listen about God's love. But even more than that, you can show them His love by setting them free, for the Kingdom of God does not consist in words but in power (1 Cor. 4:20)!

The prophet Isaiah declared that "There will be no end to the increase of His government or of peace" (Is. 9:7). That means that God's kingdom is advancing and the kingdom of darkness is diminishing. Even if it doesn't look like that to our natural eyes, that is the spiritual truth that we can count on. And you have been invited to be a part of increasing the government and Kingdom of God, and with it, peace in the hearts of men and women.

THE KINGDOM OF GOD BRINGS FORGIVENESS

But He was pierced through for our transgressions,
   He was crushed for our iniquities;
   The chastening for our well-being fell upon Him,
   And by His scourging we are healed.

All of us like sheep have gone astray,
   Each of us has turned to his own way;

But the LORD has caused the iniquity of us all
To fall on Him.   (IS. 53:5,6)

By His death and resurrection, Jesus took the punishment for our sins and reconciled us to our Father. All around you are people who are weighed down with the bondage of their sins and the horrible guilt that never stops tormenting them, reaping the wretched consequences of their own actions. They don't know that there is hope. They haven't recognized God's love for them. They don't believe there is any way out of their circumstances.

As you walk in love, you will become a living demonstration to them of God's overwhelming love for them. As you speak words of grace, you will pour healing oil into their spirits. As you share with them what God has done in you and for you, you will offer them hope that He will do the same for them.

When you have your quiet time with Jesus in two-way journaling, prayer and meditation on the Scriptures, ask Him to use you that day to touch the hurting with His love. Ask Him to open your ears to hear what He wants to say to each person you meet. Ask Him to open your eyes to see as He sees. Respond to His gentle leading throughout your day, with a word or a touch or by meeting a need. And as doors open for you to share God's love, speak as you sense Him guiding you.

There is no need to be pushy or insensitive. Rushing to speak without the Spirit preparing the heart can result in defensive walls coming up that make it harder for the person to receive the good news. Remember that one of us may sow the seed of truth, someone else may water it, and someone else bring in the harvest (1 Cor. 3:6). You are not responsible to force people to a point of decision or pressure them to say certain words. You are only responsible to be obedient to the leading of the Spirit within you.

As you are, you will share in the reward and celebrate with the angels when another soul returns home to the Father.

THE KINGDOM OF GOD BRINGS HEALING

Jesus was going throughout all Galilee, teaching in their synagogues and proclaiming the gospel of the kingdom, and healing every kind of disease and every kind of sickness among the people. (MATT. 4:23)

Heal those...who are sick, and say to them, 'The kingdom of God has come near to you.' (LK. 10:9)

He sent them out to proclaim the kingdom of God and to perform healing. (LK. 9:2)

He began speaking to them about the kingdom of God and curing those who had need of healing. (LK. 9:11)

Wherever Jesus preached the good news of the Kingdom of God, He also healed the sick. Demonstrating the love of God for His children by setting them free from their sickness, pain and disease is an integral part of proclaiming the Gospel. Even before Jesus' death on the cross, God was using physical healing to show people how much He loved them and what kind of life He wanted for them. How much more do we now offer healing since Jesus was beaten and bruised for our healing and He Himself took on our infirmities and carried our diseases (1 Pet. 2:24, Matt. 8:17).

Because you have been born again and received the gift of the Holy Spirit, you are empowered to bring healing to your world. Jesus frequently healed the sick by laying hands on them and commanding them to be healed, and He commissioned us to do the same (Mk. 16:15-18).

When you encounter someone who is sick or in pain, simply ask if you may pray for them. If they say yes, ask for their permission to touch them while you pray. If consent is given, lay your hands on the person's arm, hand, back or shoulder, as is comfortable and appropriate. Then turn your attention to Jesus, thanking Him for His love for this person and for His healing power that He has placed in you. Look to see what Jesus is doing and listen to hear what He is saying. Follow His lead as He ministers His power and grace.

THE KINGDOM OF GOD BRINGS FREEDOM

The Spirit of the Lord is upon me, because He has anointed me to preach the gospel to the poor. He has sent me to proclaim release to the captives, and recovery of sight to the blind, to set free those who are oppressed. (LK. 4:18)

If I cast out demons by the Spirit of God, surely the kingdom of God has come upon you. (MATT.12:28, LK. 11:20)

When Jesus commissioned His disciples to preach the Gospel, He assured them that if they believed, they would cast out demons (Mk. 16:17). The Spirit of the Lord is upon you and He has anointed you to preach the Gospel to the poor, to release the captives, give sight to the blind and set free those who are oppressed. What an incredible blessing it is to be given the privilege of participating in extending the Kingdom by setting people free!

Again, you must always have the permission and cooperation of the person you are praying for. If they do not want to submit themselves to the Lordship of Jesus Christ and be filled with the Holy Spirit, they are in danger of ending up in more bondage than before you prayed for them (Matt. 12:45). You must be led by the Holy Spirit as you minister deliverance. Keep the eyes of your heart on what Jesus is saying and doing so that you are working in harmony with Him, and it is His power that is manifested so that He receives all the glory for the work.

A GLORIOUS UNFOLDING!

"God's plan from the start
For this world and your heart
Has been to show His glory and His grace.
Forever revealing the depth and the beauty of
His unfailing Love,
And the story has only begun.

"And this is going to be a glorious unfolding!
Just you wait and see and you will be amazed.
We've just got to believe the story is so far from over
So hold on to every promise God has made to us
And watch this glorious unfolding."

("THE GLORIOUS UNFOLDING" BY
STEPHEN CURTIS CHAPMAN © 2013)

Your new life in Christ has just begun! You have only experienced the beginning of the love and forgiveness and power and fellowship with God that He has waiting for you. You have only tasted of His goodness and mercy and grace. The adventure is just beginning!

Living and walking by the Spirit, seeing and hearing what Jesus is doing right now and following His lead—a supernatural life is now yours. You can live the life that you thought was too good to be true. Embrace your destiny as child of God, born of the Spirit, anointed with power! And watch the glorious unfolding of the abundant life of righteousness, peace and joy that is your inheritance.

ADDITIONAL RESOURCES

- *When Heaven Invades Earth*—Bill Johnson
- *Power to Heal*—Randy Clark
- *When Everything Changes*—Steve Stewart

PERSONAL APPLICATION

1. Meditate on the following Scripture passage and let the Holy Spirit speak to you through it. What does it all mean to you, now, in your daily life?

   I pray that the eyes of your heart may be enlightened, so that you will know what is the hope of His calling, what are the riches of the glory of His inheritance in the saints, and what is the surpassing greatness of His power toward us who believe. These are in accordance with the working of the strength of His might which He brought about in Christ, when He raised Him from the dead and seated Him at His right hand in the heavenly places, far above all rule and authority and power and dominion, and every name that is named, not only in this age but also in the one to come. And He put all things in subjection under His feet, and gave Him as head over all things to the church, which is His body, the fullness of Him who fills all in all. And you were dead in your trespasses and sins...But God, being rich in mercy, because of His great love with which He loved us, even when we were dead in our transgressions, made us

*alive together with Christ (by grace you have been saved),
and raised us up with Him, and seated us with Him in
the heavenly places in Christ Jesus, so that in the ages to
come He might show the surpassing riches of His grace in
kindness toward us in Christ Jesus.*

(EPHESIANS 1:18—2:6)

----

2. Tomorrow, when you have your quiet time with Jesus in two-
way journaling, prayer and meditation on the Scriptures, ask
Him to use you that day to touch the hurting with His love.
Ask Him to open your ears to hear what He wants to say to
each person you meet. Ask Him to open your eyes to see as
He sees. Respond to His gentle leading throughout your day,
with a word or a touch or by meeting a need. And as doors
open for you to share God's love, speak as you sense Him
guiding you.

   If you are completing this study in a group, come prepared
to share your experiences.

----

3. The next time you encounter someone who is sick or in pain,
ask if you may pray for them. If they say yes, ask for their
permission to touch them while you pray. If consent is given,
lay your hands on the person's arm, hand, back or shoulder,
as is comfortable and appropriate. Then turn your attention
to Jesus, thanking Him for His love for this person and for

His healing power that He has placed in you. Look to see what Jesus is doing and listen to hear what He is saying. Follow His lead as He ministers His power and grace.

If you are completing this study in a group, come prepared to share your experiences.

_____

_____

_____

GROUP ACTIVITIES

1. Share your meditations on Ephesians together.

2. Share your testimonies of being used by God to extend His Kingdom. Rejoice together in His goodness!

3. Have a time of journaling together according to the pattern in the Group Activities of Chapter 9.

Go Deeper

Salvation Website
http://www.bornofthespirit.today/

Online Course "Your Extraordinary Life"
at
CLUSchooloftheSpirit.com/salvation
(50% off with coupon code: SALVATIONBOOK)

Also available from Mark and Patti Virkler

DIALOGUE WITH GOD
Mark and Patti Virkler

Find out how prayer—our link to God—is the most powerful and vital activity of our life. This book will lead you into a life-changing dimension of two-way communication with our loving GOD.

"Dialogue With God has dramatically changed my prayer life. I have found I can dialogue with Christ on a daily basis. I believe this inspired approach to be absolutely essential to the growth of every serious Christian."

— DR. RICHARD WATSON,
Dean of the School of Education,
Oral Roberts University

ISBN: 9780882706207

BRIDGE
LOGOS

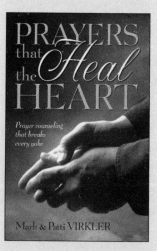

AM I BEING DECEIVED
Mark and Patti Virkler

Am I Being Deceived? answers questions like:

How can I be spiritual without becoming "New Age? "What does the Bible teach concerning visualization?How do Pharisees react to the move of the Holy Spirit?What does the Bible say about dreams, visions, and imagination?What does the Bible say about faith versus a positive mental attitude?

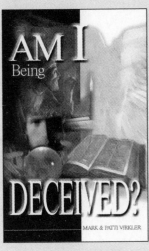

Learn the answers to these questions and many more. Get rid of the shackles that may be holding you back from true freedom and worship.

ISBN: 9780882708669

BRIDGE LOGOS